VIBE CODING FOR BEGINNERS

A Beginner's Guide to AI-Powered App Development with Generative AI

MARC MORALES

ISBN: 978-1-969899-16-4

April 2026

TABLE OF CONTENTS

Code Is Dead

Let me tell you about the funeral nobody attended. Somewhere around 2023, traditional coding as we knew it quietly flatlined in a hospital bed while the rest of the tech world was too busy arguing about cryptocurrency to notice. There were no flowers, no eulogies, and certainly no tears shed by the millions of aspiring entrepreneurs who had been told for decades that they needed a computer science degree, five years of experience, and the ability to recite Python documentation in their sleep before they could even think about building an app. The old guard of gatekeepers, those insufferable types who loved to respond to simple questions with phrases like "just read the documentation" or "have you tried Stack Overflow," suddenly found themselves watching their exclusive club membership become about as valuable as a Blockbuster rewards card.

Now before the pitchforks come out and the comment sections fill with angry developers insisting that real coding is still alive and essential, let me clarify what I mean by dead. Traditional coding, the kind that required you to memorize syntax, understand the arcane mysteries of memory allocation, and spend three days debugging a missing semicolon, has not disappeared entirely. What has died is the monopoly it held over creation. The absolute stranglehold that technical expertise once had on who could and could not bring their ideas to life has been shattered into a million pieces, and those pieces are now being swept up by anyone with a dream, a laptop, and the ability to describe what they want in plain English.

Think about this for a moment. For the entire history of software development, which admittedly is not that long in the grand scheme of human civilization but feels like an eternity in internet years, there existed an impenetrable wall between those who had ideas and those who could build them. On one side stood the dreamers, the entrepreneurs, the people who woke up at three in the morning with the perfect solution to a problem they encountered, scribbling notes on napkins and filling notebooks with wireframes and business plans. On the other side stood the developers, the engineers, the people who actually knew how to transform those napkin sketches into functional software. And between them? A wall made of syntax errors, framework dependencies, and enough technical jargon to fill a dictionary that nobody except the initiated could read.

This wall created an entire economy built on translation. Non-technical founders had to either find a technical co-founder, which often meant giving away half their company to someone who might not even share their vision, or hire expensive development agencies that charged rates making luxury car payments look reasonable by comparison. The average cost of developing a simple mobile application hovered somewhere between fifty thousand and several hundred thousand dollars, depending on complexity and how much the development agency thought they could extract from someone who did not know better. And even after spending that money, founders often ended up with something that looked nothing like what they imagined, because the process of translating human ideas into technical requirements and then into code was about as reliable as a game of telephone played across continents.

The democratization we are witnessing right now is not just an incremental improvement. It is not simply coding made slightly easier or development timelines reduced by a modest percentage. What has happened represents a fundamental restructuring of who gets to participate in the creation economy. The bar has not been lowered; it has been placed so close to the ground that you could trip over it while lying down. And this is not hyperbole or marketing speak designed to sell you on some promise that sounds too good to be true. This is the documented reality of thousands of people who have already crossed over from the "I have an idea" camp to the "I built and launched an app" camp without ever learning the difference between a function and a variable.

Consider the historical parallel. There was a time when writing and distributing content required access to printing presses, relationships with publishers, and enough capital to fund print runs that might never sell. The barrier between having something to say and actually saying it to the world was immense. Then came the internet, blogs, and social media, and suddenly anyone with thoughts could share them instantly with a global audience. Some of what emerged was garbage, certainly, but incredible voices that would have never been heard under the old system suddenly had platforms. Writers who could not have afforded a single print run became bestselling authors through self-publishing. The gatekeepers lost their power not because they disappeared but because alternative paths emerged around them.

The same revolution is happening in software development right now, and most people have not yet grasped the magnitude of what this means. Your neighbor who sells handmade jewelry could build an app to manage her customer relationships and inventory. Your uncle who has spent thirty years in the plumbing business could create a tool that helps other plumbers estimate jobs and schedule appointments. Your cousin who always complained about how hard it is to coordinate group travel could actually build the solution instead of just complaining about it during Thanksgiving dinner. The only requirement is that they can describe what they want clearly enough for an AI to understand and execute.

This accessibility has created what I like to call the Great Equalizer effect in entrepreneurship. Previously, your ability to compete in the app economy was directly proportional to your technical knowledge or your access to capital that could purchase that technical knowledge. A brilliant idea from someone in a rural town with no coding experience and limited funds was essentially worthless in practical terms. Meanwhile, a mediocre idea from someone with technical skills or venture capital backing could get built, launched, and funded regardless of whether the world actually needed it. We ended up with an app economy shaped not by the best ideas but by the ideas that happened to originate from people with the right technical or financial resources.

Now imagine the shift. Suddenly that brilliant idea from the rural town has an equal shot at existence. The playing field has not just been leveled; it has been completely rebuilt. Competition in the app marketplace is increasingly becoming a competition of ideas, execution, and marketing rather than a competition of who can afford the best development team. This is terrifying if you have built your career or business model on being a gatekeeper, and it is exhilarating if you have ever had an idea die in your head because you lacked the means to bring it to life.

The psychological impact of this shift cannot be overstated. For years, people with entrepreneurial ambitions but without technical skills walked around with what I call Idea Guilt. They felt guilty for having these ambitious dreams about apps and software because they knew they could not personally execute on them. They felt like frauds when they talked about their concepts because they knew the technical reality stood between their vision and anything tangible. Many simply stopped having ideas altogether, their creative muscles atrophying from disuse because why bother imagining solutions when you cannot build them anyway.

Software Development Will Never Be The Same

Vibe coding has cured this psychological condition for millions of people practically overnight. The realization that you can go from concept to functional prototype in an afternoon rather than six months has unlocked creative potential that was always there but suppressed by practical limitations. People are dreaming bigger now. They are allowing themselves to envision solutions to problems they encounter because the gap between imagination and creation has shrunk to nearly nothing.

But let us also address the skeptics directly, because I know they exist and I respect their position even as I disagree with it. The argument goes something like this: AI-generated code is not real development, the apps created this way are inferior, and anyone who thinks they can build serious software without understanding programming fundamentals is deluding themselves. These criticisms contain grains of truth wrapped in larger shells of misunderstanding about what most people actually need.

Here is the reality. For someone building a consumer app designed to solve a specific problem and generate revenue, the question of whether the underlying code is beautiful and optimized according to engineering best practices is largely irrelevant. Users do not care if your functions are named according to proper conventions. They do not care if your code could be more efficient. They care if your app works, solves their problem, and does not crash constantly. The standard for success in the app marketplace is not code quality; it is user satisfaction and business viability. A perfectly engineered app with no users is a failure, while a messily coded app that people love and pay for is a success by any meaningful measure.

This is not to say that code quality never matters. At scale, with millions of users and complex operations, engineering excellence becomes crucial. But the vast majority of people reading this book are not trying to build the next Instagram or compete with enterprise software companies. They are trying to build useful tools that solve real problems for real people while generating income that can range from supplementary to life-changing. For these goals, vibe coding is not just adequate; it is often optimal because it prioritizes speed to market and iteration over theoretical engineering perfection.

The paradigm shift happening here mirrors what occurred in other creative industries when technology democratized production. When digital music production tools became accessible, traditional musicians complained that bedroom producers did not understand music theory, could not read sheet music, and were creating inferior content. Some of those criticisms were valid, but they missed the forest for the trees. The democratization of music production led to entirely new genres, sounds, and successful artists who would never have emerged under the old gatekeeping system. The same pattern is emerging in app development, and the complaints from traditional developers will likely age just as poorly as the music industry gatekeepers who insisted that you needed a record deal and a recording studio to make legitimate music.

You're Still On The Ground Floor

What makes this moment particularly exciting is that we are still in the early innings of this transformation. The tools available today are incredible compared to what existed even two years ago, but they are primitive compared to what will exist two years from now. The people who recognize this shift early and begin building now, even with imperfect tools and messy results, will have massive advantages over those who wait for the technology to mature further. They will have developed intuition for how to describe software to AI, accumulated portfolios of shipped products, and built businesses while others were still debating whether this was a real trend or a passing fad.

The death of traditional coding as the only path to software creation has opened doors that were previously welded shut for most of humanity. Behind those doors lies opportunity that was historically reserved for a technical elite. The barriers that separated people with ideas from people who could execute on them have crumbled, and in their place stands nothing but possibility and perhaps a laptop and an internet connection.

As you move through the remaining chapters of this book, remember this fundamental truth: you are not learning a shortcut or a hack or a workaround for proper development. You are learning the new primary path that increasing numbers of people will take to bring their ideas to life. The traditional path will still exist for those who want it, just as acoustic guitars still exist in a world of electronic music production. But it is no longer the only path, and for many purposes, it is no longer even the best path.

The question is no longer whether you are qualified to build apps. That question assumed a technical gatekeeping system that has been dismantled. The question now is whether you have ideas worth building and the persistence to see them through to launch and profitability. Everything else, the actual construction of the software itself, has become something that can be described rather than coded, prompted rather than programmed, and vibe coded rather than hand-crafted by experts who spent years earning the right to create.

So pour one out for traditional coding as the exclusive ticket to software creation. It had a good run. It produced amazing things and made a lot of people wealthy. But its time as the only game in town has ended, and the game has opened up to everyone willing to play. The chapters ahead will show you exactly how to play this new game effectively, but first you needed to understand that the old rules no longer apply. They are dead. And something better, something more accessible, something more democratic, has risen in their place.

20

Vibe Coding for Beginners

something better, something more accessible, something more democratic, has risen in their place.

The Vibe Revolution

Let me tell you about the moment everything changed. It was not a press conference at some sleek Silicon Valley campus, nor was it a carefully orchestrated product launch with dramatic lighting and a turtleneck-clad visionary on stage. The revolution happened quietly, almost sneakily, in dorm rooms and home offices and coffee shops around the world. One day, people who had never written a single line of code woke up and realized they could build software. Real software. Apps that worked, that solved problems, that people would actually pay money to use. The technical gatekeepers who had spent decades perfecting their craft suddenly found themselves sharing the playground with absolute beginners who had nothing but ideas and the audacity to describe them out loud.

This is the vibe revolution, and if you are reading this book, you are standing at the edge of one of the most significant democratizations of creative power in human history. I know that sounds dramatic. It is dramatic. For the first time ever, the ability to create functional applications has been decoupled from the requirement to understand how they actually work under the hood. You do not need to know what an API endpoint is or why your function is throwing a null reference exception. You just need to know what you want your app to do, describe it clearly, and let artificial intelligence handle the translation from human intention to working code.

The term vibe coding itself emerged organically from the community of creators who discovered this new paradigm. It captures something essential about the process, which is fundamentally different from traditional software development. When you vibe code, you are not thinking in terms of syntax and data structures and memory allocation. You are thinking in terms of feelings, outcomes, and user experiences. You are communicating the vibe of what you want to create. You might say something like "I want a calm meditation app with soft colors that tracks how many days in a row someone has meditated and celebrates their streaks." That sentence contains no technical specifications whatsoever, yet modern AI tools can interpret it and produce a functional application that does exactly what you described.

The core philosophy behind vibe coding rests on a simple but profound insight. Human creativity and machine capability are complementary rather than competitive. For decades, we assumed that building software required humans to think like machines, learning the precise languages and logical structures that computers understand. vibe coding flips this assumption entirely. Now machines are learning to understand how humans naturally think and communicate. You bring the vision, the creativity, the understanding of human problems and desires. The AI brings the technical execution, the knowledge of programming languages and frameworks and best practices accumulated from analyzing billions of lines of code. Together, you can build things that neither of you could create alone.

This is not about replacing programmers or suggesting that traditional software engineering has no value. Professional developers remain essential for building complex systems, maintaining security, optimizing performance, and handling the countless edge cases that emerge at scale. But for the vast majority of app ideas, the ones that solve specific problems for specific groups of people, the ones that can generate meaningful income for individual creators, vibe coding provides a faster and more accessible path from concept to reality. The question is no longer whether you can build an app. The question is whether you have an idea worth building.

Replit, Cursor & Bolt – The Holy Trinity

Let's do a brief introduction of some of the tools that make this magic possible, because understanding the landscape will help you choose the right instrument for your particular symphony. The three platforms that have emerged as leaders in this space each bring their own strengths and philosophies to vibe coding and knowing when to use which tool will dramatically improve your results.

Cursor has become something of a darling among developers and vibe coding enthusiasts alike because it occupies an interesting middle ground. Built on top of Visual Studio Code, one of the most popular code editors in the world, Cursor integrates AI assistance directly into a professional development environment. When you use Cursor, you can type natural language descriptions of what you want to build, and the AI will generate the corresponding code right there in your editor. What makes Cursor particularly powerful is its ability to understand context. It sees the code you have already written, understands the structure of your project, and generates new code that fits seamlessly with what exists. For vibe coding, this means you can start with a simple prompt, get some initial code, then refine and extend it through continued conversation with the AI. You might say add a button that saves the user preferences and Cursor will not only create the button but wire it up to your existing data storage in a way that actually works. The learning curve is slightly steeper than some alternatives, but the power and flexibility you gain make it worthwhile for anyone planning to build apps seriously.

Replit takes a fundamentally different approach that prioritizes accessibility and immediate gratification above all else. This platform runs entirely in your web browser, which means you do not need to install anything or configure development environments or worry about dependencies. You simply open Replit, describe what you want to build, and watch as the AI creates a complete working application that you can test and deploy without ever leaving the browser window. Replit has invested heavily in their AI assistant, which can generate entire applications from a single paragraph description. The platform is particularly well suited for rapid prototyping and validation. If you want to test whether an idea has legs before investing significant time, Replit lets you go from concept to clickable prototype in minutes. The collaborative features also make it excellent for working with others, as you can share your projects instantly and even code together in real time. The tradeoff is that more complex applications may eventually outgrow what Replit handles elegantly, but for the majority of income-generating app ideas, it provides everything you need.

Bolt represents the newest generation of vibe coding platforms, and it pushes the boundaries of what natural language prompting can achieve. This tool specializes in generating complete, deployment-ready applications from detailed descriptions. The experience of using Bolt feels almost magical, as you describe your app in plain English, specify the features you want, explain how you imagine users interacting with it, and then watch as a full-fledged application materializes before your eyes. Bolt handles not just the core functionality but also the design, the user interface, the navigation structure, and even the basic architecture decisions that would traditionally require technical expertise to make. Where Bolt truly shines is in its ability to understand and implement relatively complex requirements from a single prompt. You can describe multi-screen applications with user accounts, data persistence, and interactive features, and Bolt will generate a coherent application that ties all these elements together. The platform also excels at creating visually polished results, producing apps that look professional rather than obviously generated.

These three platforms represent different points on the spectrum between control and convenience. Cursor gives you the most control and the closest connection to the underlying code, making it ideal for projects where you want to understand exactly what is being built and have the ability to fine-tune every detail. Replit offers a balance of power and ease, providing a complete development environment that handles all the complexity while still giving you access to the code when you need it. Bolt maximizes convenience and speed, generating complete applications with minimal input but offering less visibility into the underlying implementation. There is no universally correct choice among these options. The right tool depends on your specific project, your personal preferences, and how much you want to learn about the technical aspects of your creation.

What unites all of these platforms is their approach to the human-AI interaction. They all accept natural language input, meaning you can describe what you want in regular English sentences rather than code. They all provide iterative refinement, allowing you to see results and then request changes and improvements through continued conversation. And they all handle the translation from your intentions to working software automatically, abstracting away the need to understand programming concepts unless you choose to dive deeper.

Everyone Can Now Develop Applications

The implications of this shift extend far beyond convenience for individual creators. We are witnessing a fundamental change in who gets to participate in the creation of software. Historically, this power was concentrated among those who could afford computer science educations, those who had the time and privilege to spend years mastering complex technical skills, those who worked at technology companies with access to teams and resources. Vibe coding shatters these barriers. A single parent with an idea for an app that helps other parents can now build that app. A retired teacher who sees a better way to help students learn can now create that tool. An entrepreneur in a developing country who understands local problems better than any Silicon Valley startup can now build solutions for their community. The democratization of app creation is not just an economic opportunity. It is a profound expansion of who gets to shape the digital tools we all use.

But let us be practical as well as philosophical, because you likely picked up this book with specific goals in mind. The financial opportunity presented by vibe coding is genuine and significant. Mobile apps and web applications generate billions of dollars in revenue annually, and until now, capturing even a small piece of that revenue required either substantial technical skills or the resources to hire those who possessed them. vibe coding changes the equation by reducing the cost and time required to build apps to extreme lows. This means your potential profit margin on a successful app approaches close to 75% or more. It means you can afford to experiment with multiple ideas, launching several apps to see which ones gain traction. It means the income-generating potential of a good app idea is no longer gatekept by technical barriers.

The revolution we are experiencing is not just about making existing tasks easier. It is about making previously impossible tasks achievable. Things that would have required a team of developers working for months can now be accomplished by a single person working for hours. This compression of time and effort changes what is economically viable. Apps that would never have made sense to build because development costs would exceed potential revenue are now worth creating. Niche solutions for small audiences become profitable when they can be built in an afternoon. The long tail of app opportunities opens up in ways that were simply not possible before.

As you continue through this book, you will learn the specific techniques and strategies that transform this potential into reality. You will discover how to identify ideas worth pursuing, how to communicate effectively with AI tools, how to handle the inevitable challenges that arise, and how to turn finished apps into sustainable income streams. But none of that matters if you do not first internalize the fundamental truth that this chapter aims to convey. The technical barrier that once stood between you and app creation has been lowered to the point where it barely exists. You do not need permission from anyone.

You do not need years of education. You do not need to understand the arcane mysteries of software development. You need only an idea and the willingness to describe it clearly.

The vibe revolution invites you to participate not as a spectator but as a creator. The tools are ready. The platforms are waiting. The opportunity is unprecedented in its accessibility and potential. What remains is your decision to step through the door that has finally opened. The rest of this book will show you exactly how to make that journey successful, but the journey itself begins with a single, essential mindset shift. You are no longer someone who has app ideas. You are someone who builds apps. The only difference between those two identities is the belief that you can actually do it, and this chapter exists to eliminate any remaining doubt. The technology has caught up with your ambitions. The revolution has arrived. Now it is time to start building.

Ideas That Print

Let me tell you about the graveyard of brilliant ideas. It exists in the minds of every aspiring app developer, filled with concepts that seemed revolutionary at two in the morning but somehow never translated into a single dollar of revenue. These ideas haunt us, whispering about what could have been if only we had executed them. But here is the uncomfortable truth that nobody wants to hear: most of those ideas were never going to make money in the first place. Not because you lacked the skills to build them, especially now that vibe coding has handed you superpowers, but because the ideas themselves were fundamentally flawed from a business perspective. This chapter is about developing x-ray vision for app concepts, the ability to look at any idea and immediately understand whether it belongs in your portfolio or in that metaphorical graveyard where dreams go to decompose quietly.

The difference between apps that print money and apps that collect digital dust often comes down to a single factor that most people overlook: the problem-revenue connection. Every successful app solves a problem, but not every problem is worth solving from a financial standpoint. Consider this scenario. You notice that people often forget to water their plants, so you build a beautiful plant watering reminder app. The interface is gorgeous, the notifications are perfectly timed, and the user experience is smooth as butter. You launch it, and crickets. Not because the app is bad, but because the problem is not painful enough for people to pay money to solve it. They might download it for free, use it twice, and forget about it just like they forgot to water their plants. The lesson here is that you need to target problems that cause real pain, the kind of pain people will gladly pay to eliminate.

Research into consumer spending behavior consistently shows that people spend money in predictable categories: health, wealth, relationships, and entertainment. These four pillars have supported profitable businesses since humans invented currency, and they continue to dominate app store revenue today. When you examine the top grossing apps on any platform, you will find they almost universally fit into one of these categories. Dating apps help people find relationships. Fitness apps improve health. Finance apps grow wealth. Gaming apps provide entertainment. This is not a coincidence; it is a reflection of fundamental human priorities. Your job as an aspiring app entrepreneur is to identify specific problems within these categories that you can solve better, faster, or cheaper than existing solutions.

The Five Steps To Development Profitability

Now let us talk about the concept of problem frequency because this is where many wannabe app moguls go wrong. A problem that occurs once a year, no matter how painful, creates a terrible business opportunity. Think about apps that help you file taxes. Sure, tax filing is annoying and even scary for some people, but it happens once annually. Compare this to an app that helps people track their daily meals or manage their ongoing anxiety. These problems occur daily, sometimes multiple times per day, creating numerous opportunities for engagement and monetization. The math is simple: daily problems create daily value, which creates justification for ongoing subscriptions. Frequency multiplied by pain intensity equals revenue potential. This formula should be tattooed on the inside of your eyelids so you see it every time you close your eyes to dream up your next app idea.

Here is a framework I call the Five Filter System that has helped countless developers separate the wheat from the chaff. Every idea you consider should pass through these five filters before you invest any significant time building it. First, ask yourself whether the target audience is actually willing to spend money. Teenagers might love your app, but their wallets are controlled by parents who have different priorities. Senior citizens might need your app, but their technical adoption rates could limit your user base. Ideal targets are employed adults between twenty-five and fifty-five who control their own spending and have demonstrated willingness to pay for digital solutions. Second, consider whether the market is large enough to support your income goals. A brilliant app for left-handed clarinet players might solve a genuine problem, but the addressable market might cap your potential at a few thousand dollars annually.

The third filter examines competition, but not in the way most people think. Contrary to popular belief, no competition is actually a red flag, not a green light. When you find a problem with zero existing solutions, it usually means one of two things: either the market is too small to attract developers, or others have tried and failed because the problem cannot be profitably solved. Some competition validates that money exists in the space. What you want is competition that has weaknesses you can exploit. Maybe existing solutions are too expensive, too complicated, have terrible user interfaces, or ignore a specific segment of the market. Your competitive advantage does not need to be revolutionary; it just needs to be meaningful to your target users.

The fourth filter is what I call the explanation test. Can you explain what your app does and why someone should pay for it in a single sentence? If you cannot, you have a clarity problem that will plague your marketing efforts forever. Users decide within seconds whether to download an app, and if your value proposition requires a paragraph to communicate, you have already lost them. The apps that print money have crystal clear positioning. It helps you sleep better. It tracks your spending automatically. It teaches your kid to read. It finds cheap flights instantly. Notice how each of these statements immediately communicates the benefit without requiring additional explanation. Practice distilling your idea until you can pass this test effortlessly.

The fifth and final filter asks whether you can validate this idea for under one hundred dollars and within one week. If testing your concept requires building the entire app first, you are gambling instead of investing. The most successful app developers I know have become experts at quick validation techniques. They create simple landing pages describing the app and measure how many people try to sign up. They run small social media ads to gauge interest. They post in relevant online communities to see if the problem resonates. They interview potential users to understand their pain points and willingness to pay. All of this can happen before you write a single prompt in your vibe coding tool. The goal is to fail fast and cheap on bad ideas so you can invest your energy in ideas with validated potential.

Let me share a counterintuitive insight about finding profitable niches: the best opportunities often hide in plain sight within boring industries. While everyone races to build the next viral social media app or gaming sensation, quiet fortunes are being made in unsexy categories like inventory management for small businesses, scheduling tools for medical offices, inspection checklists for contractors, and maintenance logs for vehicle fleets. These apps rarely make headlines, but they make money consistently because they solve concrete professional problems for people who expense software costs to their businesses. A plumber who pays nineteen dollars monthly for an app that handles his invoicing does not blink at the cost because it saves him hours of administrative headaches. This is the power of targeting business problems: the return on investment is calculable and therefore easier to justify.

Speaking of professional niches, let us discuss the concept of category expertise as a competitive advantage. The best app ideas often come from identifying problems within industries you already understand. If you spent ten years as a nurse, you know the frustrations of shift scheduling and patient handoffs better than any silicon valley developer. If you ran a food truck, you understand the chaos of inventory management and location scouting in ways outsiders cannot grasp. This insider knowledge is worth its weight in gold because it helps you build solutions that actually fit how people work rather than how engineers imagine they work. Before brainstorming app ideas in random categories, inventory your own professional and personal experiences for problems worth solving. Your unfair advantage might already be sitting in your past.

You Don't Have To Be First Anymore

Now let us address the elephant in the room: originality is overrated. Some of the most successful apps in history were not first to market; they were simply better than what existed. Facebook was not the first social network. Spotify was not the first music streaming service. Uber was not the first ride-hailing app. These companies succeeded by executing familiar ideas with superior products and strategies. If you are waiting for a completely original idea that nobody has ever considered, you will wait forever. Instead, look for existing solutions that frustrate users and ask how you could make the experience ten percent better. Sometimes ten percent better is all you need to capture meaningful market share, especially in underserved niches where the bar for quality is embarrassingly low.

Trend spotting represents another powerful technique for identifying profitable opportunities. New technologies, regulations, cultural shifts, and demographic changes constantly create fresh problems that need solving.

When remote work exploded in 2020, suddenly millions of people needed tools for home office productivity, virtual team collaboration, and work-life balance. When cryptocurrency entered mainstream consciousness, opportunities emerged for portfolio trackers, tax calculators, and educational apps. When AI became accessible, a wave of AI-powered tools flooded every category imaginable. Your job is to watch for these shifts and identify the secondary problems they create. Every major trend spawns dozens of smaller problems that fly under the radar of big companies but represent perfect targets for nimble solo developers using vibe coding tools.

The validation process deserves deeper exploration because it separates serious entrepreneurs from dreamers. Start by identifying where your potential users already congregate online. Reddit communities, Facebook groups, LinkedIn networks, Discord servers, and specialized forums are goldmines for understanding real problems and testing concepts. Spend time reading what people complain about, what questions they ask repeatedly, and what workarounds they have created for unsolved problems. These complaints and questions represent potential app ideas wrapped in market research. When you think you have spotted an opportunity, engage with the community. Ask questions about their pain points. Propose your solution and gauge reactions. This qualitative research costs nothing but time and provides invaluable insights that no amount of abstract theorizing can match.

Quantitative validation adds another layer of confidence before you commit to building. Tools like Google Keyword Planner show you how many people search for solutions to specific problems each month. App Store Optimization tools reveal the search volume for various keywords within the stores themselves. Social listening platforms track conversations about topics across the internet. This data helps you estimate market size and demand without relying solely on intuition. If nobody is searching for solutions to the problem you want to solve, that silence tells you something important. Conversely, if thousands of people search monthly for help with a specific issue and existing solutions have mediocre ratings, you may have found a sweet spot worth pursuing.

Let us talk about the minimum viable concept versus the feature bloat trap. When you fall in love with an idea, your brain naturally starts adding features. What if it also did this? And what about integrating that? Before you know it, your simple app idea has transformed into a complex ecosystem that would take months to build and confuse users upon arrival. The apps that print money typically do one thing exceptionally well before expanding. Instagram initially was just photo filters and sharing. WhatsApp was just messaging. Mint was just expense tracking. They added features over time based on user demand, not upfront speculation. When validating ideas, focus on the core value proposition and resist the temptation to solve every adjacent problem simultaneously. You can always add features later if users request them.

Finally, consider building a systematic approach to idea generation rather than waiting for inspiration to strike. Set aside time weekly to review trending apps, read industry news, browse startup databases, and explore what problems people discuss in online communities. Maintain an ideas list that you regularly review and evaluate against the frameworks discussed in this chapter. Rate each idea on problem frequency, pain intensity, market size, competition landscape, and validation feasibility. This disciplined approach ensures you always have multiple concepts in various stages of development, reducing the pressure to make any single idea work. The best app entrepreneurs are not geniuses who strike gold once; they are systematic thinkers who generate, evaluate, and test ideas continuously until they find winners worth scaling.

The journey from random idea to income-generating app begins with this critical evaluation phase. Many people skip it because they are excited to start building, and vibe coding makes building so easy that the temptation intensifies. But building the wrong app quickly is not actually progress; it is just faster failure. Take the time to filter your ideas through rigorous analysis. Validate before you create. Target problems that hurt enough to justify payment, occur frequently enough to sustain engagement, and exist within markets large enough to support your financial goals. When you combine this strategic thinking with the vibe coding superpowers you have already acquired, you become genuinely dangerous in the best possible way: someone who can identify opportunities others miss and execute on them faster than traditional developers can even spec out requirements. That combination is how ordinary people build extraordinary income streams in the app economy, one well-chosen idea at a time.

Vibe Coding Platforms

If you have ever stared at a blank screen wondering how on earth you were supposed to transform your brilliant app idea into something real without spending years learning traditional programming, then congratulations, you have found your tribe. Vibe coding represents a fundamental shift in how we approach software development, and the platforms we will explore in this chapter serve as your trusty vehicles on this creative journey. Think of them as different modes of transportation, each with their own strengths, quirks, and ideal use cases. Some are sports cars built for speed, others are comfortable sedans perfect for longer journeys, and a few might best be described as those quirky little scooters that somehow get you exactly where you need to go while making you smile the entire way.

All The Top AI Platform Players

Let us begin with Replit, a platform that has earned its reputation as the Swiss Army knife of coding environments. Replit operates as a browser-based integrated development environment, which is a fancy way of saying you can write, run, and deploy code without installing anything on your computer. For vibe coders creating mobile applications, this accessibility factor cannot be overstated. You could be sitting in a coffee shop with a borrowed laptop, struck by sudden inspiration for a meditation timer app, and within minutes you could have a working prototype running in your browser. The platform supports an impressive array of programming languages and frameworks, but more importantly for our purposes, it has embraced AI-assisted development with open arms. When you start a new project on Replit, you can describe what you want to build in plain English, and the platform's AI assistant will help generate the foundational code. Setting up Replit requires nothing more than creating a free account, and you can upgrade to paid tiers if you need more computational resources or want to keep your projects private. The platform truly shines when you need to experiment rapidly, collaborate with others in real-time, or build projects that require server-side functionality alongside your mobile interfaces. If your app idea involves any kind of backend processing, user authentication, or database storage, Replit offers a cohesive environment where all these pieces can live together harmoniously.

Moving along to Cursor, we encounter a platform that has carved out a special niche by reimagining what a code editor can be in the age of artificial intelligence. Cursor is essentially a supercharged text editor that lives on your desktop, and it has been designed from the ground up to work alongside AI as your coding partner. For vibe coders, this means you can highlight a section of code you do not quite understand, ask for an explanation in plain language, and receive clear guidance without needing to context-switch to documentation or tutorial websites. The setup process for Cursor involves downloading the application to your computer and connecting it with your preferred AI service, which typically means entering an API key or signing into an integrated service. Where Cursor absolutely excels is in scenarios where you want more control over your development environment and need to work with existing codebases. Perhaps you have found a mobile app template online and want to customize it extensively, or maybe you are building something that requires integration with local tools and files on your machine. Cursor handles these situations with grace, offering intelligent code completion and generation while respecting the established patterns in your project. The platform rewards users who invest time in learning its shortcuts and features, making it an excellent choice for vibe coders who plan to develop multiple applications over time and want a tool that grows with their skills.

Now we arrive at Bolt.new, a platform that has generated considerable excitement in the vibe coding community for its remarkable ability to transform natural language descriptions into functional applications with stunning speed. When you visit Bolt.new, you are greeted with a simple prompt interface that invites you to describe the application you want to build. Type something like "create a mobile-friendly habit tracking app with a clean dark theme and the ability to mark habits complete with satisfying animations," and watch as the platform generates not just code, but a fully functional preview you can interact with immediately. The magic of Bolt.new lies in its streamlined approach to the creation process. There is no setup to speak of, no accounts required to start experimenting, and no complex configuration to navigate. You simply describe, generate, iterate, and deploy. This makes Bolt.new absolutely ideal for vibe coders who want to validate ideas quickly or create standalone utilities that do not require extensive backend infrastructure. The platform works best for frontend-focused applications, meaning projects where the primary functionality happens in the user's browser or on their device rather than requiring server-side processing. If you are building a calculator, a timer, a visualization tool, or any application where the logic can run entirely client-side, Bolt.new will serve you remarkably well. However, if your vision involves user accounts, saved data across sessions, or real-time synchronization between multiple users, you may need to pair Bolt.new with additional services or consider one of our other platform options.

Windsurf has emerged as a compelling option for vibe coders who appreciate a balance between accessibility and power. Like Cursor, Windsurf functions as an AI-native code editor, but it has been designed with a particular focus on flow states and minimizing friction during the creative process. The platform takes its name seriously, aiming to help developers glide through their projects with the same effortless momentum one might experience riding wind currents across water. Setting up Windsurf follows a similar pattern to other desktop-based tools, requiring a download and installation process followed by configuration of your AI preferences. What distinguishes Windsurf is its thoughtful approach to context awareness.

The platform maintains an understanding of your entire project, not just the file you are currently editing, which allows for more intelligent suggestions and fewer interruptions when working on interconnected components of your mobile application. Vibe coders building medium to large applications will find Windsurf particularly valuable when they need to modify functionality that spans multiple files or when refactoring existing code to accommodate new features. The platform also includes robust debugging assistance, helping you understand why something is not working and offering concrete solutions rather than leaving you to puzzle through error messages alone. For mobile application development specifically, Windsurf integrates well with popular frameworks and can help you navigate the sometimes confusing landscape of cross-platform development tools.

Lovable represents a delightfully different philosophy in the vibe coding platform landscape. The name itself signals the platform's priorities, focusing on creating applications that people genuinely enjoy using and that developers enjoy building. Lovable emphasizes design quality and user experience as first-class concerns, recognizing that the best functionality in the world means little if users find an application confusing or unpleasant to interact with. When you begin a project on Lovable, you will notice that the platform guides you to think about visual design, user flows, and interaction patterns alongside the technical implementation. This makes it an outstanding choice for vibe coders building consumer-facing mobile applications where aesthetics and usability directly impact success. Setting up Lovable involves creating an account and familiarizing yourself with its unique interface, which blends visual design tools with AI-assisted code generation in ways that feel almost like collaboration with a design-minded colleague. The platform particularly shines for applications in the lifestyle, social, and creative tool categories, where users expect polish and attention to detail. If your mobile app idea involves any kind of personal branding, visual portfolio elements, or targets audiences who appreciate thoughtful design, Lovable deserves serious consideration as your development platform of choice.

Base44 takes yet another approach, positioning itself as a platform for building full-stack applications with remarkable speed using AI assistance. The name evokes the concept of a foundation, a base upon which you can construct sophisticated applications without needing to understand every layer of the underlying technology stack. For vibe coders, Base44 offers an appealing combination of power and accessibility. The platform handles many of the complex decisions around architecture, database design, and API structure, allowing you to focus on describing what you want your application to do rather than how it should technically accomplish those goals. Getting started with Base44 involves account creation and a brief onboarding process that helps the platform understand your project goals. Where Base44 truly excels is in scenarios requiring user data persistence, authentication systems, and the kind of backend functionality that transforms simple applications into genuinely useful tools. If your mobile app needs to remember user preferences across sessions, store user-generated content, or enable interactions between different users, Base44 provides the infrastructure to make these features possible without requiring you to become an expert in database management or server administration. The platform works exceptionally well for productivity applications, social tools, and any mobile app where data continuity matters.

Claude Artifacts, offered through Anthropic's AI platform, takes a minimalist approach that surprises people with its effectiveness. You describe what you want, and Claude generates functional code artifacts that you can run directly. The tight feedback loop between conversation and execution makes it particularly good for learning because you can ask why something works the way it does and receive explanations alongside working code.

FlutterFlow deserves inclusion because it specifically targets mobile app development with a visual approach. You design interfaces by dragging and dropping components, and AI assists with the logic and integration aspects. The learning curve is gentle, the results are genuinely native mobile apps, and the community has produced extensive resources for common use cases.

Firebase Studio, Google's entry into this space, integrates tightly with Google's cloud infrastructure. If you envision building apps that scale to millions of users or require sophisticated backend services, starting with Firebase Studio sets you up with infrastructure that handles growth gracefully. The initial experience is more complex than simpler tools, but the architecture it establishes pays dividends as applications expand.

Finally, we come to Vercel, a platform that occupies a unique position as both a deployment destination and a development environment. While some of the other platforms we have discussed focus primarily on the creation phase, Vercel has built its reputation on making the deployment and hosting of web applications remarkably straightforward. For vibe coders building mobile web applications, understanding Vercel is essential because it often serves as the final step in bringing your creation to the world. The platform offers automatic builds, global distribution, and performance optimizations that would require significant expertise to implement independently. Setting up Vercel involves connecting it to your code repository, which might live on GitHub or another version control service, and configuring a few deployment settings. Once configured, Vercel can automatically deploy new versions of your application whenever you make changes, providing a seamless path from code to live product. The platform integrates beautifully with modern web frameworks that are popular for mobile development, including Next.js, which Vercel actually created and maintains. For vibe coders planning to build progressive web applications, which are web-based applications that can be installed on mobile devices and behave much like native apps, Vercel provides an excellent hosting foundation. The platform also offers edge functions and serverless capabilities for those whose applications require some server-side processing, bridging the gap between purely frontend solutions and full-stack infrastructure.

Understanding which platform to choose for your specific mobile application idea requires honest assessment of several factors. Consider first the complexity of your data requirements. Applications that need to remember things, whether user preferences, created content, or interaction history, generally require backend infrastructure and databases, pointing you toward platforms like Replit, Base44, or Vercel combined with another creation tool. Next, evaluate your design priorities. If your application lives or dies by its visual appeal and user experience, Lovable's design-first approach may serve you well. Think about your development style preferences too. Do you prefer working in a browser without installing anything, or do you want the power and customization options of a desktop application? Bolt.new and Replit offer browser-based experiences, while Cursor and Windsurf provide desktop environments with deeper system integration. Consider also whether you are building a one-off project or establishing a workflow for ongoing development. Platforms like Cursor and Windsurf reward investment in learning their features, making them excellent choices for vibe coders committed to creating multiple applications over time.

As you embark on your vibe coding journey, remember that these platforms are tools rather than destinations. The most successful vibe coders often develop familiarity with multiple platforms and select the right tool for each specific project. You might prototype quickly in Bolt.new, migrate to Replit when you realize you need backend functionality, and deploy the finished product through Vercel. This flexibility represents one of the great advantages of the current moment in software development. The barriers that once separated "real programmers" from everyone else have crumbled, replaced by a landscape of accessible tools that meet creators where they are and help them build what they imagine. Your job is simply to start, to choose a platform that resonates with your first project idea, and to begin the delightful process of bringing your mobile application visions to life. The platforms will be there to support you, and this book will guide you through seventy-five specific examples of what you can create. But first, pick a platform, create an account, and take that essential first step. Your vibe coding adventure awaits.

Your First App

Let me tell you something that would have made my computer science professor spit out his coffee back in 2015. You are about to build a fully functional mobile app today. Not next month. Not after completing a bootcamp. Today. Right now. In the time it takes to watch a Marvel movie, you will have created something real, something that works, something you can actually show people and eventually sell. If that sounds impossible, I completely understand. I felt the same way the first time someone showed me these tools. I kept waiting for the catch, the fine print, the moment when everything would fall apart and reveal that yes, you still need to understand recursive algorithms and memory management and all those things that make normal people run screaming from programming. That moment never came.

The app we are going to build together is a simple but genuinely useful habit tracker. I chose this particular project for several reasons. First, habit tracking apps consistently rank among the most downloaded categories in both app stores, which means there is proven market demand. Second, the features involved touch on most of the core functionality you will need for any app you build in the future including data storage, user interface design, notifications, and basic logic. Third, and this is the selfish reason, habit trackers are actually useful. By the end of this chapter, you will have something you might genuinely want to use yourself, which makes the whole process feel less like homework and more like building something meaningful.

Back In My Day Of App Development…

Before we dive into the actual building process, let me paint you a picture of what traditional app development used to look like. A developer would first need to decide whether they were building for iOS or Android, which is like choosing which half of your potential customers you want to ignore. They would then download several gigabytes of development software, configure their environment which often took days to get right, learn a programming language like Swift or Kotlin, understand the specific architecture patterns each platform requires, figure out how to design interfaces that follow platform guidelines, implement data persistence, handle background processes, and then repeat the entire process for the other platform. The average solo developer working nights and weekends might ship a basic app after three to six months of dedicated work. The average corporate development team might take even longer because meetings exist.

Now let me tell you what we are going to do instead. We are going to describe what we want in plain English, watch the AI generate the code, preview it instantly, make adjustments through conversation, and have a working prototype within a couple of hours. The technology stack, the architecture decisions, the syntax errors, all of those traditional headaches become somebody else's problem. Or more accurately, they become the AI's problem, and unlike human programmers, the AI does not charge by the hour or need coffee breaks.

Get Your Hands Dirty Right Now

Open up your laptop and navigate to one of the vibe coding platforms. This can be done on a mobile phone as well, but for your first app you should probably use a larger screen so you can see and feel the weight of what you're doing. For this tutorial, I am going to assume you are using Replit because it offers a fantastic free tier and the mobile app deployment features are especially beginner friendly.

Create an account if you have not already, and start a new project. When prompted for what you want to build, you are going to enter your first real vibe coding prompt. This is where everything we discussed in the prompting chapter comes into play. Type something like this:

I want to build a mobile habit tracker app where users can create daily habits, mark them complete each day, and see their streak counts. The design should be clean and minimal with a calming color palette. Include a way to add new habits, delete habits, and view weekly progress.

Watch what happens next. The AI begins generating code, creating files, establishing the structure of your application. You will see file names appear that you do not need to understand. You might notice terms like components and state management and API routes. Ignore all of that for now. What matters is the preview window where your app is materializing out of thin air like some kind of digital sorcery. Within a minute or two, you will see the basic interface. There will be a place to add habits, a list showing any habits you have created, and some kind of visual indication of progress. It will look rough. It will probably look like a programmer designed it, which historically has not been a compliment. But it works. Click around. Add a test habit. Mark it complete. Refresh the page and watch your data persist. You just built an app.

Now comes the fun part. This is where vibe coding transforms from a neat trick into an actual superpower. Start talking to the AI about improvements. Tell it you want the complete button to have a satisfying animation when tapped. Tell it you want the color scheme to shift to navy blue and gold because those colors feel more premium. Tell it you want a celebration modal to appear when a user hits a seven day streak. Each request generates new code, updates existing files, and the preview refreshes to show your changes. You are designing and developing simultaneously through nothing but conversation. This is what makes vibe coding feel like cheating. Traditional development separates planning, design, and implementation into distinct phases with different skill sets and often different team members. vibe coding collapses all of that into a single fluid dialogue.

But let me give you some real talk here because I want this book to prepare you for actual success, not just theoretical possibility. Your first prompt will not produce a perfect app. Your second round of instructions might break something that was working before. The AI will sometimes interpret your requests in unexpected ways, like the time I asked for a dark mode toggle but I didnt know it was actually called "dark mode". I described something else and it literally added a flashlight feature that turned the phone's actual light on and off. Hilarious in retrospect, frustrating in the moment. The key is remembering that iteration is the process. You are not failing when you need to make corrections. You are developing. That back and forth conversation between you and the AI is exactly how professional developers work with these tools. The difference is they might spot issues faster because of their experience, but they are going through the same fundamentally conversational process.

Spend about an hour refining your habit tracker. Add features that excite you. Maybe you want habits to have different frequencies, some daily and some weekly. Maybe you want to earn points for consistency that unlock different themes. Maybe you want to share streaks with friends. Each feature request teaches you more about how to communicate effectively with the AI and gives you a better sense of what is possible. By the time you finish this session, you will have created something that genuinely looks and feels like a real app. Not a toy. Not a demo. A real piece of software that solves a real problem.

Look at what you built. Really look at it. A few hours ago, this was nothing but a vague idea. Now it exists. It functions. It could theoretically be installed on someone's phone and help them build better habits. That transformation from idea to reality used to require months of study followed by months of development. You just collapsed that timeline into an afternoon. This is not about replacing programmers or devaluing technical skills. Plenty of applications require deep expertise and always will. But an enormous category of useful applications, the kind of apps that solve specific problems for specific audiences and generate legitimate income for their creators, those apps no longer require that expertise. The bar has been lowered so dramatically that the only remaining requirement is having an idea worth building and the willingness to sit down and build it.

Your habit tracker is version one. It works but probably needs polish before anyone would pay for it. That is expected and normal. The beautiful thing about vibe coding is that improvement happens through the same conversational process. Tomorrow you could spend another hour adding a widget feature. Next week you could implement cloud sync so users can access their habits across devices. Each session builds on the last, and the app grows in capability while your skills in guiding the AI grow alongside it.

You just did something that would have been impossible for a non-programmer to accomplish five years ago. Let that sink in. The technology barrier that separated people with ideas from people who could execute those ideas has crumbled. You are now standing in the rubble, holding a working application, ready to build whatever comes next.

Coding Considerations

Let me tell you something that might save your app, your sanity, and possibly your entire vibe coding career. While the magic of describing what you want and watching AI build it feels like having a genie in your laptop, there are some foundational concepts that even the most powerful AI cannot think about for you. These are the guardrails, the safety nets, and frankly, the stuff that separates apps that actually work in the real world from apps that look great in a demo and then burst into flames the moment real users touch them.

Now before you panic and think this chapter is about to turn into a computer science lecture that makes your eyes glaze over, take a breath. We are not going to make you memorize anything or write code from scratch. What we are going to do is give you the mental models and awareness you need to have intelligent conversations with your AI coding partner. Think of this as learning enough about cars to know that putting sugar in the gas tank is bad, without needing to become a mechanic. You do not need a degree in these topics, but you absolutely need to know they exist and why they matter.

Don't Forget Authentication & Authorization

Let us start with something that will affect every app you build that has users or at least requires data confidentiality, which is authentication. Authentication is just a fancy word for how your app knows who someone is. When you log into your banking app and it asks for your email and password, that is authentication. When you tap that little button that says Sign in with Google or Continue with Apple, that is also authentication. Here is why this matters enormously for you as a vibe coder. If you build an app where users can create accounts, save data, or access anything personalized, you need authentication. And getting authentication wrong is not like getting the button color wrong. Getting authentication wrong means strangers can access other people's private data, hackers can waltz into accounts they do not own, and you could end up with legal problems that make app store rejection look like a pleasant afternoon.

The good news is that vibe coding platforms and AI tools know about authentication and can implement it for you. The key is that you need to tell them you need it and specify what type you want. Do you want email and password login? Social login with Google and Apple? Magic link authentication where users get an email with a clickable link? Each has tradeoffs. Email and password is familiar to everyone but means you are storing passwords, which adds responsibility. Social login is convenient and offloads security to the big companies, but some users are paranoid about connecting their Google account to random apps. Magic links feel modern and eliminate password problems but require users to have access to their email every time they want to log in.

When you prompt your AI assistant to build your app, specifically mention authentication early. Something like "I need users to be able to create accounts and log in using their email and a magic link for password-less authentication," will get you much better results than adding user accounts as an afterthought. Authentication touches almost everything in your app, so retrofitting it later is like trying to add a foundation to a house that is already built.

Databases: Development VS Production

Now let us talk about something that has destroyed more apps and caused more founder heart attacks than almost any other beginner mistake, which is the difference between development databases and production databases. This is absolutely critical, so lean in close.

When you are building your app, you are working in what we call a development environment. This is your sandbox, your playground, your place to experiment and break things without consequences. Your development database is full of fake users named Test User and John Doe, sample data you created while building features, and probably some embarrassing entries you made at two in the morning when you were tired and testing things with names you would not want your mother to see.

Your production database is sacred ground. This is where your real users live. Their actual accounts, their real data, their payment information, their uploaded photos, their carefully crafted profiles. This is the database your live app connects to after you ship it to the app stores.

Here is where people get into trouble. In the excitement of building and testing, it is incredibly easy to accidentally point your app at the wrong database. Maybe you are testing a feature that deletes user accounts and you accidentally run it against production. Congratulations, you just deleted all your real users. Maybe you are experimenting with a data migration and you corrupt your production database. Your app is now broken for everyone, and you are scrambling to restore from a backup that may or may not exist.

The solution is to always, always, always keep these environments separate. When you are prompting your AI to build features, be explicit about which environment you are working in. Create clear separation in your configuration. Most vibe coding platforms handle some of this automatically, but you need to understand it is happening. Before you run any command that modifies data, ask yourself am I absolutely certain this is pointing at my development database and not production? That moment of pause could save your entire business.

Secret Keys & The Importance Of Not Sharing

This brings us naturally to environment variables, which sound technical but are actually a beautifully simple concept that will protect you from countless disasters. Environment variables are like labeled drawers where you keep sensitive information and configuration settings that change depending on where your app is running.

Imagine you have a house key, a car key, and an office key. You do not just throw them all in a pile and grab randomly. You label them and keep them organized. Environment variables work the same way. Your database connection information, your API keys for services like payment processing or email, your secret codes that authenticate your app with third party services, all of these live in environment variables.

Why does this matter? First, security. If you accidentally share your code publicly or push it to a repository someone can access, your environment variables are stored separately and stay protected. Without this separation, you might accidentally publish your database password to the entire internet, which is about as fun as it sounds. Second, flexibility. Your development environment uses a different database than production, remember? With environment variables, you just swap out the values when you deploy without changing any code.

When working with AI tools, you will often see them create files with names like .env or reference things like process.env.DATABASE_URL. These are your environment variables at work. Pay attention when your AI mentions them, make sure you understand what each one does, and never, ever share them publicly or commit them to version control.

Frontend VS Backend

Now let us shift gears and talk about something that affects how your users actually experience your app, which is the difference between frontend and backend. Understanding this distinction will make you a dramatically more effective vibe coder because you will know what questions to ask and how to structure your prompts.

The frontend is everything your user sees and touches. The buttons, the screens, the animations, the colors, the way text appears, the form where they enter their email. When someone says your app looks beautiful, they are talking about the frontend. The backend is everything that happens behind the curtain. When a user taps a button to save their profile, the backend receives that request, validates the data, stores it in the database, and sends back a confirmation. When your app needs to fetch a list of products or calculate a user's subscription status, the backend does that work.

Why does this matter for vibe coding? Because when something goes wrong or does not work as expected, knowing whether it is a frontend or backend problem helps you troubleshoot effectively. If a button looks wrong or is in the wrong position, that is frontend. If a button looks right but nothing happens when you tap it, that could be frontend failing to send the request or backend failing to process it. If data is not appearing that should be there, it might be a backend issue fetching the data or a frontend issue displaying it.

When you describe problems to your AI assistant, being specific about where you think the issue lives gets you faster solutions. The save button exists but when I tap it nothing saves is much more useful than the app is broken. The user profile shows blank even though the database has data in it tells the AI to look at how the frontend is fetching and rendering information.

This is also why some apps feel faster than others. A well-designed app does smart things like showing optimistic updates on the frontend while the backend processes in the background, caching data so it does not need to fetch everything fresh every time, and loading critical content first while less important things load lazily. When you are prompting your AI to build features, thinking about this user experience can help you request implementations that feel snappy and professional.

Speaking of user experience, let us discuss UI design basics because even though you are not a designer, the choices you make about how your app looks dramatically affect whether people use it or delete it within thirty seconds.

The most important principle in UI design is consistency. If buttons on one screen are blue and rounded, they should be blue and rounded everywhere. If tapping a card opens a detail view, every card should work that way. Users build mental models of how your app works, and inconsistency forces them to relearn things constantly, which feels frustrating even if they cannot articulate why.

Hierarchy matters enormously. The most important thing on each screen should be the most visually prominent. If you have a screen where users need to tap a Buy Now button, that button should not be hiding in a corner or competing with twelve other equally sized elements. Make important things big, obvious, and impossible to miss.

White space is your friend. Beginners often try to cram everything onto every screen, but cluttered interfaces feel overwhelming and cheap. Give your elements room to breathe. Professional apps use generous padding and spacing, and that simple practice elevates perceived quality dramatically.

When prompting your AI, you can reference design systems and patterns. Saying something like use a clean minimal design with plenty of white space and a clear visual hierarchy gives much better results than just make it look nice. You can also reference apps that have the aesthetic you want. Something like I want the navigation to feel similar to how Instagram handles their bottom tab bar gives your AI a concrete example to learn from.

Something WILL Break, So You Break It First

Now here is a consideration that many new vibe coders overlook until it bites them, which is error handling and edge cases. When you are building and testing your app, you naturally do things the correct way. You enter valid email addresses, you fill out all the required fields, you tap buttons once and wait patiently. Your users will literally do none of these things.

Users will double tap buttons and try to submit forms twice. They will enter email addresses without the at symbol. They will try to upload profile pictures that are actually videos. They will lose internet connection halfway through a transaction. They will rotate their phone while a screen is loading. They will find every possible way to do something you never anticipated.

Good apps handle these situations gracefully. When you prompt your AI to build features, specifically ask about error handling. What happens if the user enters invalid data? What should show if the network request fails? How do we prevent duplicate submissions? What does the user see while something is loading? These questions separate apps that feel solid from apps that feel brittle and unfinished.

Another crucial consideration is data validation, which ties into both security and user experience. Validation means checking that data is correct and appropriate before accepting it. This happens on the frontend to give users immediate feedback when they make mistakes, and it happens on the backend because you can never trust data that comes from the outside world.

If your app has a field for phone numbers, validation should ensure users actually enter something that looks like a phone number. If there is a profile bio with a character limit, validation should enforce that limit. If users are uploading files, validation should check file types and sizes. Without validation, users accidentally enter garbage data, intentional troublemakers enter malicious data, and your database fills with inconsistent information that causes problems down the road. Also, if you are utilizing user authentication, usernames or display names for user profiles should have a scheme and avoid problematic characters. I promise you, if you don't take these things into consideration you'll find out the hard way when your live users force you to consider the possibilities.

The State Of The App Union

We should also discuss state management, which sounds intimidating but is really just about keeping track of what is happening in your app at any given moment. Is the user logged in or logged out? Is this screen loading, showing content, or displaying an error? Has the user already seen the onboarding tutorial? Is there unsaved work that would be lost if they navigate away?

State gets complicated because it can exist in multiple places. Some state lives on the server and is the source of truth for things like user profiles and saved data. Some state lives temporarily on the device and tracks things like which tab is currently selected or what the user has typed into a form before submitting. When state gets out of sync between these places, weird things happen. Users see stale data, updates seem to not save, and the app feels buggy and unreliable.

When building features with AI, think about what state each feature needs and where that state should live. If you are building a shopping cart, does the cart persist on the server so users can access it from multiple devices, or does it only live locally? These decisions have implications for complexity, user experience, and what happens in edge cases like app crashes or users logging out.

Finally, let us talk about technical debt, which is not money you owe anyone but rather a metaphor for shortcuts and imperfect solutions that accumulate over time. When you are moving fast, you will often take the quick path to get something working. Maybe you copy and paste similar code instead of creating a reusable component. Maybe you hardcode values that should be configurable. Maybe you skip adding proper error handling because you want to see the feature work first.

All of these shortcuts are fine in moderation, but they add up. Eventually the quick hacks make your app harder to change, more likely to break, and more confusing to work with. The AI can help you clean things up, but you have to know that cleanup is needed. Periodically ask your AI to review code for improvements, refactoring opportunities, and best practices you might have missed in the rush to ship.

The beautiful reality of vibe coding is that you do not need to be an expert in any of these areas. You need to be aware they exist, understand why they matter, and know enough to guide your AI partner toward good decisions. Think of yourself as the architect and the AI as the construction crew. You do not need to know how to pour concrete yourself, but you definitely need to know that buildings require foundations.

Every concept covered in this chapter represents real situations where new vibe coders have launched apps that failed, lost user data, or created security nightmares. By understanding these fundamentals, you are building on a solid foundation that will support everything you create. The excitement of vibe coding is absolutely warranted, but that excitement paired with foundational awareness is what transforms hobbyists into entrepreneurs who build apps that actually work, actually scale, and actually generate the life-changing income you are pursuing.

Prompt Mastery

Let me tell you something that took me an embarrassingly long time to figure out. The difference between someone who builds amazing apps with AI tools and someone who spends three frustrating hours getting a broken mess of code has almost nothing to do with technical skill. It has everything to do with how you talk to the machine. I know that sounds like I am oversimplifying things, but stick with me here because this chapter might just be the most valuable thing you read in this entire book.

Think about the last time you asked someone to do something and they completely missed the mark. Maybe you told your friend to grab you a coffee and they came back with some oat milk monstrosity when you clearly wanted a regular latte with two sugars. Except you did not actually say any of that out loud. You assumed they would just know. We do this constantly with other humans, and we do it even more with AI tools. The problem is that AI does not have the benefit of knowing you for years, reading your body language, or understanding your unspoken preferences. It only has exactly what you type into that prompt box. Nothing more, nothing less.

The art of prompt mastery is essentially learning to communicate with radical clarity while simultaneously giving your AI collaborator enough context to make intelligent decisions on your behalf. It sounds simple when I put it that way, but mastering this skill separates the people who build profitable apps in a weekend from the people who rage quit and go back to scrolling social media.

Tell The AI Who It's Building For

Here is the first advanced technique that will immediately improve your results. I call it the persona prime, and it works like magic. Before you even describe what you want built, you need to tell the AI who it is supposed to be while building it. Instead of jumping straight into asking for a login screen, you start by establishing context. You might say something like you are an expert mobile app developer who specializes in clean, modern user interfaces and has fifteen years of experience building authentication systems that users actually enjoy using. Now you need to help me create a login screen for my fitness tracking app.

Why does this work so well? Because AI models have been trained on millions of examples of code and text written by everyone from complete beginners to world class engineers. When you tell it to adopt a specific persona, you are essentially filtering its responses through the lens of that expertise. The code you get back when you ask an expert to help you will be dramatically different from what you get when you just throw a request into the void.

Trauma Dumping On Your AI Agent

The second technique builds on this foundation and I have seen it transform the output quality for people who were ready to give up on vibe coding entirely. I call it the context dump, and it involves front loading your prompt with an almost excessive amount of information about your project. Most people make the mistake of being too brief. They type make me a shopping cart feature and then wonder why the AI produces something generic and unusable. Instead, you want to paint a complete picture before making your request.

A properly contextualized prompt might explain that you are building a sustainable fashion marketplace app where users can buy and sell secondhand designer clothing.

Your target users are environmentally conscious millennials and Gen Z consumers who care about authenticity verification and want a premium but not pretentious experience. The app already has user profiles with saved payment methods and a messaging system for buyers and sellers. Now you need a shopping cart feature that fits this aesthetic and allows users to save items, see estimated shipping costs, and checkout with their saved payment method or add a new one.

Do you see how much more the AI has to work with now? It understands the vibe of your app, who will be using it, what already exists, and specifically what you need. The output will be tailored rather than generic. It will probably even include thoughtful touches you did not explicitly request because the AI can now make intelligent inferences about what would serve your users well.

When To Be Nit-Picky

The third technique addresses one of the most frustrating aspects of working with AI tools, which is when you get code that works but does not quite match your vision. I call this iterative refinement, and it requires a mindset shift. Instead of trying to get everything perfect in a single prompt, you approach your AI collaborator the way you would approach a talented junior developer on your team. You give clear feedback, make specific requests for changes, and build toward your vision through conversation.

When something comes back and it is close but not right, resist the urge to start over. Instead, tell the AI exactly what you like and exactly what needs to change. You might say that the overall structure is perfect and you love how the buttons are laid out, but the color scheme is too dark for your brand and you need the checkout button to be more prominent. Also the font size on the item names is too small for older users and you want to make sure accessibility is prioritized throughout.

This approach saves massive amounts of time because you preserve what is working while fixing what is not. Starting over with a completely new prompt often leads you in circles where you fix one problem but lose something that was working before. Treat your prompts like a conversation, not a series of independent requests.

Constraints Are Our Friends

Now let me share a technique that sounds counterintuitive but produces remarkable results. I call it the constraint canvas, and it involves deliberately limiting the AI rather than giving it free rein. You might think that more freedom would lead to better creativity, but the opposite is often true. When you tell the AI it can do anything, it defaults to generic patterns and common solutions. When you give it specific constraints, it has to think harder and often produces more innovative results.

Try including constraints like building this feature using only the components that already exist in your app without adding any new libraries. Or tell it to create this interface using a maximum of three colors and ensuring it works perfectly on a small four inch screen. These limitations force the AI to be creative within boundaries, and the results are often cleaner and more cohesive than what you get from open ended requests.

No Means No, Most Of The Time

Another powerful technique involves what I call negative prompting, which means explicitly telling the AI what you do not want. This is especially useful if you have been burned by certain patterns in the past or have strong preferences about how your app should work. You might specify that you do not want any pop up modals because they annoy your users, or that you should never use infinite scroll because your app deals with discrete categories that users need to navigate intentionally.

The AI does not know about that one time an autoplaying video made you throw your phone across the room, but it will respect your boundaries if you articulate them clearly. Building a list of your do not want items and including them in relevant prompts can save you countless revision cycles.

Let me talk about something that trips up almost everyone when they start vibe coding, which is the assumption that longer prompts are always better. There is absolutely a sweet spot, and going past it can actually hurt your results. If your prompt becomes a full essay, the AI can lose track of what is actually important versus what is just context. The key is to be comprehensive but focused.

I recommend structuring your prompts in three mental sections even though you write them as flowing text. First comes the context, where you establish who you are, what your app is about, and what already exists. Second is the specific request, where you clearly state what you need built. Third is the parameters, where you include any constraints, preferences, or specific requirements. Keeping these sections roughly balanced tends to produce the best results.

Here is a technique that will save you from the most common frustration in vibe coding, which is when the AI gives you code that looks right but breaks in ways you cannot understand. I call it the test spec, and it involves asking the AI to tell you how to verify its work before you even run the code. After any significant feature request, add a line asking the AI to explain how you will know if this is working correctly and what you should see when you test each function.

This does two powerful things. First, it forces the AI to think through edge cases and potential failure points while writing the code, which often leads to more robust output. Second, it gives you a roadmap for verification so you are not just clicking around randomly hoping things work.

Another advanced move involves leveraging the AI understanding of design patterns and best practices without needing to know the technical terms yourself. You can simply describe the behavior you want and ask the AI to implement it using whatever approach experienced developers would consider the standard solution. This prompt pattern signals that you want professional quality code without requiring you to know that you should specifically ask for something like the repository pattern or dependency injection.

Tell The AI To Check Itself, Trust Me

The technique I want to share next has generated more surprise and delight among people I have taught than almost any other. It involves asking the AI to critique its own work before you even look at the output. After your main request, add something like now review what you just created and tell me about any potential issues, areas for improvement, or things you would do differently if you were starting over.

This self reflection prompt often surfaces problems that would have taken you hours to discover through testing. The AI might mention that the current approach would not scale well if you get more than a hundred users, or that there is a potential security concern with how data is being handled. You get senior developer level code review for free, built right into your prompt.

Speaking of security, there is a prompting pattern specifically for ensuring your app does not have embarrassing vulnerabilities. When working on anything involving user data, payments, or authentication, explicitly ask the AI to implement this feature following security best practices and then explain what security measures you included and why. This makes security an explicit requirement rather than hoping it gets included by default.

Let me address the elephant in the room, which is that sometimes the AI just gets things completely wrong no matter how good your prompt is. When this happens, do not keep rephrasing the same request hoping for different results. Instead, try what I call the decomposition approach, where you break your big request into smaller independent pieces.

If asking for a complete social media feed feature is producing chaos, step back and ask first for just the data structure to represent a post. Then ask for the visual component to display a single post. Then ask for the scroll behavior and loading logic. Assembling these pieces yourself gives you more control and often produces a better result than trying to get everything at once.

The most successful vibe coding entrepreneurs I know have developed what I call a prompt library, which is essentially a collection of their most effective prompts organized by function. When they need to build a new feature, they do not start from scratch every time. They grab a proven prompt template and customize it for their current project. Building this library takes time, but it compounds in value because every good prompt you develop accelerates all your future work.

Finally, I want to emphasize the mindset that makes all these techniques actually work in practice. You need to approach AI as a collaboration rather than a transaction. The people who struggle see prompting as pushing a button and waiting for a result. The people who thrive see it as having a conversation with an incredibly capable but sometimes literal minded partner.

When you adopt the collaboration mindset, you stop being frustrated when things need refinement. You start being curious about how to communicate better. You celebrate when you discover a prompting pattern that works well and you immediately document it for future use. You recognize that getting better at prompting is a skill that directly translates into being able to build better apps faster, which translates into more income and more freedom.

The techniques in this chapter represent thousands of hours of collective experimentation by the vibe coding community. Some of these patterns emerged from machine learning research papers. Others were discovered by solo developers at two in the morning who just needed their stupid button to work correctly. All of them are proven to improve your results when applied consistently.

Start incorporating these techniques one at a time. Do not try to revolutionize your prompting approach overnight. Pick one technique, use it for a week until it becomes automatic, then add another. Within a month, you will be getting results that would have seemed impossible when you started. Within three months, you will be helping other people understand why their prompts are not working and what they should do differently.

The secret weapon of successful vibe coding is not talent or luck or even having the best app ideas. It is the ability to translate the vision in your head into language that an AI can act upon effectively. Master this skill and you master the entire game.

Debug Like Pro

Something broke. The screen that was supposed to display your beautiful user dashboard now shows a cryptic message that looks like it was written by a robot having an existential crisis. Your heart sinks. Your palms get sweaty. Mom's spaghetti. Just kidding, but seriously, this moment right here is where most aspiring vibe coding entrepreneurs throw in the towel, slam their laptop shut, and convince themselves that maybe they were never meant to be app developers anyway. But here is the truth that separates those who build life-changing income from those who just talk about it at dinner parties: errors are not failures. Errors are conversations. They are your app trying to tell you something, and once you learn how to listen, you will realize that debugging is less like defusing a bomb and more like being a detective in a really nerdy mystery novel.

Let me paint you a picture that every vibe coder will recognize eventually. You spent the last two hours crafting what you thought were perfect prompts. The AI understood your vision. It generated beautiful code that you could not write yourself in a million years. You hit that run button with the confidence of someone who just parallel parked on the first try. And then nothing works. Or worse, something partially works, which is honestly more confusing than complete failure. The login button takes you to a blank page. The data you entered vanishes into the digital void. The app crashes every time someone tries to upload an image. Welcome to the club, friend. Every single developer who has ever shipped an app has stood exactly where you are standing right now, staring at something that does not work and wondering if they accidentally angered the technology gods.

The beautiful irony of vibe coding is that the same AI tools that build your app are also your most powerful debugging partners. This is where things get genuinely exciting, because traditional debugging required you to understand the code well enough to find the problem yourself. That meant learning to read stack traces, understanding memory allocation, knowing the difference between null and undefined, and about a thousand other technical concepts that made debugging feel like performing surgery while blindfolded. vibe coding flips this entire paradigm on its head. You do not need to understand why the code is broken in technical terms. You just need to describe what is happening versus what should be happening, and let the AI do the heavy lifting.

Debugging Doesn't Have To Be Complicated

Here is your first and most important debugging technique, and I want you to tattoo this on your brain: copy the error message exactly as it appears and paste it directly to your AI assistant with context about what you were trying to do. That is it. That is the whole technique. It sounds almost insultingly simple, but this single habit will solve roughly seventy percent of your problems without any additional effort. Error messages are not random gibberish designed to mock you. They are actually very specific descriptions of what went wrong, written in a language that AI understands perfectly even when you do not. When you see something like TypeError undefined is not a function at line 247, you might as well be reading ancient Sumerian. But your AI assistant looks at that message and immediately knows that somewhere in your code, something tried to use a value that does not exist as if it were a function.

The key to making this work is providing context. Do not just throw an error message at your AI and expect miracles. Tell it what you were trying to accomplish when the error occurred. Explain what the user was doing, what button they clicked, what screen they were on. Describe what you expected to happen versus what actually happened. This context transforms a generic error into a specific puzzle that the AI can actually solve. Think of it like calling a doctor. You would not just say you feel bad and expect a diagnosis. You would say you have been having sharp pains in your lower back that started after you tried to move that couch by yourself, and they get worse when you bend over. That specificity helps the doctor understand your situation. Same principle applies here.

Now let us talk about the different categories of problems you will encounter, because understanding what type of issue you are facing helps you communicate more effectively with your AI debugging partner. The first category is syntax errors, and these are actually the easiest to fix because the AI can spot them instantly. Syntax errors are basically typos in the code structure, like a missing comma, an extra bracket, or a quotation mark that never got closed. The good news is that most vibe coding environments will highlight these errors before you even run your app, and a simple copy paste to your AI will result in an immediate fix.

The second category is logic errors, and these are trickier because the code runs without crashing but does not do what you wanted. Your app works, technically speaking, but the calculations are wrong, the data flows to the wrong place, or features behave in unexpected ways. These require you to be more descriptive with your AI. You need to explain the expected behavior in detail. If your tip calculator should show fifteen percent of the bill but instead shows fifteen times the bill, telling the AI that specific discrepancy helps it identify where the math went sideways.

The third category is integration errors, and these happen when different parts of your app fail to communicate properly. Maybe your login system works perfectly in isolation, but the user information never makes it to the profile screen. Maybe your payment processing succeeds, but the purchase is never recorded in your database. These errors require you to describe the flow of data through your app, explaining what happens at each step and where the chain breaks. Integration errors often hide in the spaces between features, in the handoffs and data passes that connect your various app components.

The fourth category is environment errors, and these are the sneakiest of all because they might not even involve your code directly. These are problems with settings, configurations, API keys, permissions, and the various external services your app connects to. If your app works perfectly in the development environment but fails when you try to test it on a real device, you are probably dealing with an environment issue. If features that require internet access fail silently, check your network permissions and API configurations. The AI can help you audit these settings, but you need to provide information about where and how the error occurs.

Let me share a debugging technique that professional developers use religiously, adapted for the vibe coding workflow. It is called rubber duck debugging, and the original version involves explaining your problem out loud to a rubber duck sitting on your desk. The act of articulating the problem forces you to think through it systematically, and often you discover the solution while explaining it. In vibe coding, the AI is your rubber duck, except this duck actually talks back with helpful suggestions. When you encounter a stubborn bug, try writing out a complete explanation of the problem as if you were telling a story. Start from the beginning. Explain what the feature is supposed to do, how you built it, what prompts you used, and exactly when and how things started going wrong. This narrative approach often reveals assumptions you made that were not valid or steps you might have missed.

Another powerful technique is the process of elimination. When something breaks and you are not sure why, start disabling parts of your app one by one until the problem disappears. If you just added three new features and suddenly your app crashes on startup, disable two of them and see if it still crashes. If it does, the problem is in the remaining feature. If it does not, re-enable one of the disabled features and test again. This systematic approach narrows down the culprit without requiring you to understand the technical details of what went wrong. Once you identify which feature is causing the problem, you can provide that focused information to your AI for a much more targeted fix.

There is also what I call the fresh eyes technique, which is surprisingly effective and requires zero technical knowledge. When you have been staring at a problem for too long, your brain starts filling in gaps and making assumptions that might not be accurate. Step away from the computer for fifteen minutes. Take a walk. Make some coffee. Do something completely unrelated. When you come back, read through your prompts and the AI responses with fresh perspective. You might notice something obvious that you missed while you were deep in the frustration tunnel. Alternatively, try explaining your problem to another person, even someone with zero technical background. The act of simplifying your explanation often reveals the solution hiding in plain sight.

Don't Let Bugs Break You

Now let us address the emotional component of debugging, because this is where many people actually fail. When something breaks, especially something you have invested time and hope into, it triggers a stress response. Your brain goes into fight or flight mode, which is exactly the wrong state for problem solving. You start catastrophizing, imagining that your entire app is fundamentally broken, that you wasted all this time, that maybe your idea was stupid to begin with. I need you to recognize this spiral when it starts and consciously interrupt it. Take a deep breath. Remind yourself that every working app you have ever used went through this exact same process. The developers who built your favorite games, social media platforms, and productivity tools all stared at error messages and felt the same frustration you are feeling right now. The only difference is they kept going.

Here is a mindset shift that changed everything for me: start thinking of bugs as features you have not finished building yet. When something breaks, it means you have discovered an edge case or scenario that your initial prompts did not account for. This is actually valuable information. It means your app is teaching you about its own requirements. Each bug you fix makes your app more robust, more reliable, and more ready for real users. The apps that achieve the highest ratings and generate the most revenue are not the ones that never had bugs. They are the ones whose developers found and fixed the bugs before users encountered them.

You should also know that some problems are not bugs at all but rather miscommunications between you and the AI about what you actually wanted. Sometimes the AI builds exactly what you asked for, but what you asked for was not what you meant. When you encounter behavior that seems wrong, ask yourself honestly whether you described that feature precisely enough. Did you specify what should happen in edge cases? Did you explain how this feature should interact with other parts of your app? Did you provide examples of input and expected output? Going back to refine your original prompts is not admitting failure. It is recognizing that communication is a two-way process and improving your side of the conversation.

As you gain experience debugging, you will start recognizing patterns. You will notice that certain types of features tend to produce certain types of errors. You will develop intuition about where to look when something goes wrong. This accumulated knowledge is incredibly valuable, and I encourage you to keep notes about problems you encounter and how you solved them. Create a personal troubleshooting guide that you can reference when similar issues appear in future projects. This documentation practice transforms frustrating experiences into valuable assets for your app development business.

Let me leave you with this final thought on debugging that I hope you carry with you throughout your vibe coding journey. Every error message is just a conversation starter. The AI is not judging you when something breaks. It is not keeping score of how many mistakes you make. It is simply waiting to help you find the solution, which it will do tirelessly, patiently, and without any of the frustration you might be feeling. Your job is not to be perfect or to never encounter problems. Your job is to keep the conversation going until the app works. The developers who build life-changing income are not the ones who avoid errors. They are the ones who have learned that errors are just part of the process, temporary obstacles on the road to a finished product that serves users and generates revenue.

So the next time something breaks, and it will break because that is just how software development works, I want you to smile. Not a sarcastic frustrated smile, but a genuine one. Because you now know that this error is not the end of your project. It is just the next step. Copy that error message, add your context, and let the AI help you fix it. Then move on to the next feature, the next challenge, the next opportunity to build something amazing. That is how you debug like a pro, not by having all the answers but by knowing how to find them.

Ship It Fast

Let me tell you about the moment I almost threw my laptop out of a third-story window. There I was, sitting in my home office at two in the morning, staring at yet another cryptic rejection email from Apple. My app, which worked perfectly on my phone, had been denied for the fourth time in three weeks. The reason? Something about metadata inconsistencies that I still do not fully understand to this day. Meanwhile, my Google Play submission had been stuck in review limbo for what felt like an eternity. I had built an amazing app using vibe coding tools in a matter of hours, yet here I was, weeks later, still unable to get it into the hands of actual users. That experience taught me something valuable, something I am now going to share with you so that you never have to contemplate defenestrating expensive electronics.

The publishing process has historically been the final boss of app development, the dragon guarding the treasure after you have already slain all the other monsters. Traditional developers often joke that building the app is the easy part. Getting it through the maze of app store requirements, provisioning profiles, certificates, and review guidelines is where dreams go to die. But here is the beautiful truth that most people in the vibe coding space do not talk about enough. The same tools and approaches that simplified building your app can also dramatically streamline the publishing process. You just need to know the shortcuts, understand the system, and approach it with the right strategy.

Let us start with the cold hard reality of what you are dealing with. Apple and Google are the gatekeepers to billions of potential users and, by extension, billions of dollars in revenue. They take their gatekeeper role seriously, sometimes too seriously if you ask anyone who has ever received a rejection for having a button that was three pixels too close to the edge of the screen. Apple reviews every single app that gets submitted to their store, and they employ actual humans to do it. Google has automated much of their review process, which means faster approvals but also sometimes bizarre rejections that make you question whether a robot truly understands the purpose of your meditation timer app. Understanding these two different philosophies is crucial to navigating both ecosystems successfully.

Surprise, It's Pay To Play

The first step in your publishing journey happens long before you are ready to submit anything. You need developer accounts, and this is where you should not cut corners or procrastinate. Apple charges $99 per year for their Developer Program membership, and Google charges a one-time fee of $25 for their Play Console access. Here is the trick that will save you days of waiting. Sign up for both accounts the moment you start building your app, not when you finish it. Apple's enrollment process can take anywhere from a few hours to a few days depending on their verification backlog and whether you are registering as an individual or an organization. I have seen people finish their app in an afternoon only to wait a week for Apple to approve their developer account. Do not be that person. Get these accounts set up immediately, even if your app is nothing more than a vague idea and some optimistic prompts.

For Apple specifically, you will need to decide whether to enroll as an individual or as an organization. If you are just getting started and testing the waters, individual enrollment is simpler and faster. You will use your personal name as the seller name on the App Store, which is fine for most purposes. If you already have a business entity or you want a company name displayed instead of your personal name, organization enrollment requires additional verification including a DUNS number, which is essentially a business identification number from Dun and Bradstreet. Getting a DUNS number is free but can add another week or two to your timeline. Plan accordingly.

Now let us talk about the actual submission process, starting with Google Play because it is generally the friendlier of the two platforms for first-time publishers. Google Play Console has evolved significantly over the years, and they have actually put effort into making the process more intuitive. When you upload your app, you will need to provide a bunch of information including your app description, screenshots, a feature graphic, a privacy policy URL, and various declarations about your app's content and data practices. The privacy policy requirement trips up a lot of first-time publishers. You absolutely need one, even if your app does not collect any user data whatsoever. There are free privacy policy generators online that can create a basic compliant policy in minutes. Just search for app privacy policy generator and pick one that lets you specify exactly what data your app does or does not collect.

Screenshots are another area where vibe coding developers often stumble. You need high-quality screenshots that showcase your app's best features, and Google requires specific dimensions for different device types. Here is a shortcut that works beautifully. Use your vibe coding tool or a simple AI image tool to help you create mockups and screenshots. Many of these tools can generate device frames around your screenshots, add promotional text, and make your listing look professional without you needing any graphic design skills. The quality of your screenshots directly impacts your conversion rate, which is the percentage of people who view your listing and actually download your app. Do not skimp on this step.

The App Stores' Review Process

Google's review process typically takes anywhere from a few hours to three days, though they state it can take up to seven days. In my experience, simple apps with no special permissions usually clear review in under twenty-four hours. Apps that request sensitive permissions like camera access, location data, or access to contacts will receive additional scrutiny and take longer. If your app genuinely needs these permissions, make sure you have clear explanations ready for why. If you added them during development but do not actually use them, remove them before submitting. Unnecessary permission requests are one of the fastest ways to trigger extended review times and potential rejections.

Apple's App Store Connect is a different beast entirely. The interface is sleeker but the requirements are stricter, and the review process is more thorough. Apple prides itself on the quality and security of apps in their ecosystem, which is great for users but can be frustrating for developers. Before you can even submit to Apple, you need to understand the world of certificates, provisioning profiles, and identifiers. This is traditionally where non-technical people hit a wall so high they can see the curvature of the Earth from its base. Here is the good news. Modern vibe coding platforms and tools like Expo, Flutter with various build services, and even Replit's mobile capabilities have abstracted away much of this complexity. If you are using one of these platforms, follow their specific documentation for iOS deployment. They often handle certificate management automatically or provide step-by-step wizards that make the process much less painful than doing it manually.

For those who do need to wrangle certificates manually, here is the simplified version. You need an App ID which identifies your app, a distribution certificate which proves you are you, and a provisioning profile which connects your app to your certificate and specifies where and how it can be distributed. Apple has different types of provisioning profiles for development, ad hoc distribution, and App Store distribution. For publishing, you need the App Store distribution profile. Creating these through the Apple Developer portal can feel like navigating a maze designed by someone who actively dislikes you, but there are numerous tutorials and videos that walk through each step. Take your time, follow the instructions exactly, and do not be afraid to delete everything and start over if things get tangled up. I have done that more times than I care to admit.

Once your app is actually built and signed correctly, App Store Connect submission requires similar information to Google but with additional requirements. Apple demands app preview videos for certain categories, specific screenshot dimensions for each device type you want to support, and detailed explanations of how various features work. They also have age rating questionnaires and content descriptions that must be filled out accurately. Lying or misrepresenting your app's content is a fast track to rejection and potentially having your developer account suspended. Not worth it.

Apple's review process typically takes between twenty-four hours and three days, though this can vary wildly depending on the time of year, their current backlog, and the complexity of your app. The weeks leading up to major holidays tend to have longer review times, so plan accordingly if you are trying to launch a seasonal app. Apple's reviewers will actually use your app, so make sure any demo accounts or test scenarios are clearly documented in the review notes section. If your app requires a login, provide a test account with pre-populated data. If certain features require specific conditions to test, explain exactly how to trigger them. The easier you make the reviewer's job, the smoother your approval will go.

Rejections happen, and when they do, the key is not to panic. Read the rejection reason carefully, even if it makes your blood pressure spike. Apple provides specific guideline references with each rejection, so look up those guidelines and understand exactly what they are asking for. Most rejections fall into a few common categories. Crashes and bugs are obvious. Insufficient metadata usually means your screenshots do not match your actual app or your description is misleading. Guideline violations can range from requiring users to sign in before they can see any content to including references to competing platforms to not having a clear enough business model. That last one has become more common recently because Apple wants to know how free apps make money and wants their cut of any digital goods sold within the app.

The appeals process exists for rejections you believe are unjust, but use it sparingly and professionally. Apple's review team is made up of humans who read your appeals personally. A well-written, respectful explanation of why you believe your app complies with guidelines can sometimes result in a reversal. An angry rant about how unfair they are being will not help your case and may actually hurt your relationship with the review team. Pick your battles, make substantive changes when the feedback is legitimate, and save appeals for genuine misunderstandings.

Here is a strategy that has saved me weeks of time over my publishing career. Submit your app for review before it is perfect. Apple and Google allow you to submit apps for review and then release them manually whenever you are ready. This means you can have your app sitting in an approved state while you continue tweaking your marketing materials, preparing your launch strategy, or fixing minor issues that do not affect the core functionality. Once approved, you can release at the push of a button. This is particularly valuable if you are trying to coordinate a launch with a marketing campaign or a specific date.

Build testing into your timeline, but not in the way you might expect. Both platforms offer testing programs that let you distribute your app to a limited group before full public release. Apple has TestFlight, which allows you to invite up to ten thousand testers. Google has internal testing, closed testing, and open testing tracks. Use these religiously. Beyond finding bugs, having even a small group of testers gives you early feedback on confusing interfaces, missing features, or performance issues on devices you do not own. It also gives you people who might leave early positive reviews when you do launch publicly, which can be incredibly valuable for your app store optimization.

The timeline for getting from finished app to live in both stores can realistically be as short as three to five days if you have your accounts set up, your materials prepared, and you follow the guidelines correctly on your first submission. Most people take longer because of preventable issues. Missing privacy policies, incorrect screenshot dimensions, and cryptic build errors add days. Rejections for minor issues add more days. The fastest publishers are the ones who have been through the process before and know exactly what both platforms expect. By reading this chapter, you are now one of those people. You know about the privacy policy requirement before it surprises you. You know to set up developer accounts early. You know to use testing tracks and to submit for review before you are completely ready to launch.

The app stores are not obstacles designed to keep you out. They are gateways to millions of potential users who have already entered their credit card information and are actively looking for apps that solve their problems. Understanding the rules of the game does not make you a sellout. It makes you smart. The vibe coding revolution has done something remarkable by eliminating the technical barriers between your idea and a working app. Now you have the knowledge to eliminate the logistical barriers between that working app and real users downloading it on their phones. The playing field has never been more level.

Go ship something. The stores are waiting, and so are your future customers.

Money Machines

Let me tell you a secret that separates the hobbyists from the entrepreneurs in the app world. Building something amazing means absolutely nothing to your bank account if you do not have a clear path to getting paid. I have seen countless developers, both traditional coders and vibe coding pioneers, create genuinely useful applications that sit on the app stores collecting digital dust while generating precisely zero dollars. These creators made the critical mistake of treating monetization as an afterthought, something to figure out later, when in reality it should be woven into the DNA of your app from the very first prompt you type into your AI tool.

The beautiful irony of the vibe coding revolution is that while the technical barrier to building apps has collapsed to nearly nothing, the business fundamentals remain exactly the same as they have always been. Your app needs to solve a problem, reach people who have that problem, and extract value in exchange for the solution. The technology changed, but human psychology and the laws of commerce remain stubbornly constant. This chapter is about building money machines, not just apps. We are going to dive deep into the mechanisms that transform your creation from a clever project you show your friends into a legitimate income stream that can change your financial trajectory.

You Will Want To Entertain Subscriptions

The subscription model has become the darling of the app economy for excellent reasons that go beyond simple greed. When you build an app that charges users on a recurring basis, whether monthly or annually, you create something magical called predictable revenue. Predictable revenue lets you sleep at night, plan for the future, and invest in growth because you know approximately how much money will arrive in your account next month. Compare this to the anxiety-inducing roller coaster of one-time purchases where you constantly need new customers just to maintain your income. Subscriptions create a business while one-time purchases create a transaction.

Now here is where things get interesting for vibe coders specifically. The types of apps that justify subscriptions typically fall into categories where ongoing value is obvious and continuous. Think about productivity tools that people use daily, fitness apps that provide new workouts each week, meditation apps with expanding content libraries, or utility apps that require server resources to function. If your app delivers fresh value over time or requires infrastructure that costs you money to maintain, subscriptions make logical sense to your users. They understand they are paying for ongoing access to something that keeps getting better or keeps requiring resources to operate.

The psychology of subscription pricing deserves your attention because getting it wrong can torpedo an otherwise excellent app. Research consistently shows that users have specific price sensitivity thresholds that trigger different mental reactions. A subscription under five dollars monthly registers as trivial for most smartphone owners in developed markets. Between five and ten dollars requires the user to perceive meaningful value but remains an impulse decision. Above ten dollars monthly and you have entered serious consideration territory where users will actively compare your offering against alternatives and their own needs. The sweet spot for most solo vibe coders breaking into the market sits in that four to seven dollar monthly range, or better yet, somewhere around thirty to fifty dollars annually when offered as a discounted yearly option.

Speaking of annual subscriptions, always offer them and always make them feel like a deal. The standard playbook is to price your annual subscription at roughly the cost of eight to ten months of the monthly rate. This accomplishes two critical objectives simultaneously. First, it dramatically increases customer lifetime value because annual subscribers stick around much longer than monthly subscribers who might cancel after their first impulsive sign-up. Second, it gives you cash upfront that you can reinvest into marketing, improvements, or simply enjoying life while your app works for you.

The freemium model deserves special consideration because it pairs beautifully with the vibe coding approach to rapid development and iteration. Freemium means giving away a functional version of your app for free while reserving premium features, content, or capabilities for paying users. This model works because it eliminates the biggest barrier to user acquisition, which is asking someone to pay for something they have never experienced. Users can download your app, fall in love with it, integrate it into their lives, and then encounter a natural moment where upgrading feels like the obvious choice rather than a hard sell.

The art of freemium design lies in finding the perfect balance between generosity and restraint. Give away too much and users have no reason to upgrade. Give away too little and users never experience enough value to care about getting more. The winning formula typically involves letting users accomplish their core objective with the free version while making that accomplishment significantly easier, faster, or more enjoyable with premium features. Think about photo editing apps that let you edit for free but watermark exports unless you pay, or task management apps that work great for individuals but require payment to collaborate with teams.

Is Ad Revenue Worth The Hassle?

Advertising revenue represents the most accessible monetization method for vibe coders because implementation requires minimal technical expertise and users have been trained by decades of free, ad-supported software to accept the tradeoff. When you monetize through advertising, your users pay with their attention rather than their wallets, and advertisers pay you for access to that attention. The math is straightforward enough that anyone can understand it. You earn money based on impressions, which means ads being shown, and clicks, which means users interacting with those ads. Rates vary wildly based on your user demographics, geographic location, and the type of ads you display.

Banner ads sit at the bottom of the revenue potential ladder but also at the bottom of the user annoyance ladder. These small rectangular ads typically earn between one and three dollars per thousand impressions, meaning you need serious volume to generate meaningful income. Interstitial ads, those full-screen advertisements that appear between screens or activities, earn considerably more but also irritate users considerably more. The highest earning format is rewarded video ads, where users choose to watch a short video advertisement in exchange for in-app benefits. These can earn anywhere from ten to forty dollars per thousand completions and users actually appreciate them because they feel like a fair exchange rather than an interruption.

The dirty secret of advertising monetization is that it requires massive scale to generate life-changing income. If your app earns three dollars per thousand ad impressions and you want to make five thousand dollars monthly, you need to generate over one and a half million ad impressions every single month. That translates to tens of thousands of active daily users, which is achievable but requires serious marketing effort or a genuinely viral app concept. Advertising works best as a supplementary revenue stream for most solo developers or as the primary model for apps targeting enormous markets with casual, frequent usage patterns like games, weather apps, or simple utilities.

Hybrid monetization strategies combine multiple approaches and often outperform any single method. The most common and effective hybrid pairs freemium with advertising, offering users a free ad-supported experience that can be upgraded to a premium ad-free experience. This captures revenue from users who will never pay for anything while also capturing premium revenue from users who value their attention and experience enough to eliminate advertisements. You effectively segment your user base into two groups and optimize revenue extraction from each.

Paying Once And Being Done

One-time purchases still have their place in the app economy, particularly for apps that deliver complete, finished value without ongoing content updates or server requirements. Games with defined endings, specialized tools that solve permanent problems, or reference apps with static content can justify asking users to pay once for permanent access. The psychological advantage of one-time purchases is simplicity and transparency. Users know exactly what they are paying and exactly what they are getting, which can accelerate conversion rates compared to subscriptions that feel like ongoing commitments.

The challenge with one-time purchases is the treadmill effect I mentioned earlier. Once someone buys your app, they become a former customer rather than a current subscriber. Your revenue directly correlates with new customer acquisition, which means your marketing can never stop. Successful one-time purchase developers often build portfolios of related apps, creating ecosystems where users who enjoyed one purchase become likely buyers of future releases. This portfolio approach transforms the treadmill into more of a flywheel where each new app benefits from the audience built by previous apps.

Choosing the right monetization strategy for your specific app requires honest assessment of several factors. First, consider your target audience and their relationship with money and time. Budget-conscious users in price-sensitive markets respond better to ad-supported free apps. Professional users solving business problems often prefer paying for premium tools that respect their time and present professionally. Second, examine your app category and what users already expect. Fitness apps have normalized subscriptions, games have normalized in-app purchases and ads, and productivity tools have normalized both subscriptions and one-time purchases depending on complexity.

Third, and this is crucial for vibe coders specifically, consider your own capacity for ongoing development and content creation. Subscriptions create expectations of continuous improvement and fresh content. If you plan to build your app and move on to the next project, forcing users into subscriptions feels dishonest and generates cancellations and negative reviews. One-time purchases or ad support might align better with a build-and-move-on philosophy. Conversely, if you genuinely plan to improve and expand your app continuously, subscriptions align your incentives with your users because you only get paid if you keep them happy enough to keep paying.

The technical implementation of monetization through vibe coding tools has become remarkably straightforward. When prompting your AI development assistant, you can directly request integration with services like RevenueCat for subscription management, AdMob for advertising, or built-in purchase capabilities provided by Apple and Google. The AI understands these services and can generate the necessary code to connect your app to payment processing infrastructure. You will still need to configure accounts with Apple, Google, and any third-party services, but the actual coding work that used to require specialized knowledge now happens through natural language conversation.

Testing your monetization before committing matters more than most developers realize. Both Apple and Google provide sandbox environments where you can process fake purchases to ensure everything works correctly before going live. Take advantage of these tools ruthlessly. Nothing destroys user trust faster than payment issues, failed subscriptions that still charge, or features that remain locked despite successful purchases. Test every purchase path, every restore purchase scenario, and every edge case you can imagine before a single real user encounters your payment flows.

Pricing psychology extends beyond the numbers themselves into how you present them. The way you frame your pricing dramatically impacts conversion rates, and understanding a few key principles can multiply your revenue without changing your actual prices. Anchoring works by presenting your most expensive option first, making subsequent options feel more reasonable by comparison. Most apps show their annual subscription prominently positioned above the monthly option, making the monthly price feel expensive and the annual price feel like a smart deal. Charm pricing, using numbers ending in nine or seven, still works in the app economy just as it works everywhere else. An app priced at $4.99 monthly feels meaningfully cheaper than one priced at $5.00 monthly even though the difference is literally one cent.

Social proof in pricing comes from showing users that others have already made the purchase and experienced positive outcomes. Phrases like joined by over fifty thousand subscribers or most popular choice next to a pricing tier leverage our deep psychological tendency to follow the crowd. You cannot fabricate these numbers, but once you have legitimate traction, displaying it prominently near your purchase prompts increases conversion rates significantly.

The timing of your monetization pitch matters enormously. Hitting users with upgrade prompts before they have experienced value generates instant resentment and app deletions. The optimal moment to request payment arrives immediately after a user has experienced a win or breakthrough using your app. They completed a workout, created something beautiful, solved a problem, or achieved a goal. In that moment of positive emotion and demonstrated value, your upgrade prompt transforms from an annoyance into a natural next step. vibe coding makes implementing these smart triggers remarkably easy. Simply describe to your AI assistant the user action or milestone that should trigger your premium offering, and the logic gets built into your app automatically.

Remember that monetization is not a one-time decision but an ongoing experiment. The data your app generates about user behavior, upgrade rates, cancellations, and feature usage tells a story about what your users actually value. Listen to that story and iterate accordingly. You might discover that a feature you considered premium is actually essential for user retention and should become free. You might find that users would happily pay more for a specific capability you undervalued. The vibe coders who build sustainable income streams treat their monetization strategy as a living system that evolves based on evidence rather than assumptions.

The ultimate money machine is not any single app but rather the skills, systems, and audience you build along the way. Each app you launch teaches you something about what users want, what they will pay for, and how to reach them. Each successful monetization validates your instincts and builds confidence for bigger bets on future projects. The vibe coding revolution has not just lowered the bar for building apps. It has lowered the bar for running experiments that used to cost tens of thousands of dollars in development time. Now you can test monetization hypotheses in days instead of months, learning at a pace that was previously impossible for individual creators.

Your money machine awaits assembly. The components are well understood, the tools are accessible, and the only remaining variable is your willingness to build, test, and iterate until you find the combination that works for your unique app and audience. The developers generating life-changing income from apps are not smarter than you. They simply started earlier and failed forward faster. With vibe coding eliminating the technical barriers that used to slow iteration cycles, you can compress years of learning into months. The question is no longer whether you can build an app that makes money but rather how quickly you can discover the specific formula that unlocks revenue from your creation.

Users On Demand

Let me tell you the most uncomfortable truth in the app business, one that countless brilliant developers have learned the hard way after months of painstaking work. You could build the most revolutionary, beautifully designed, perfectly functional app the world has ever seen, and it will sit in the app store gathering digital dust while generating exactly zero dollars if nobody knows it exists. This is not pessimism talking. This is mathematics. Zero users multiplied by any monetization strategy equals zero income, and all the vibe coding magic in the world cannot change basic arithmetic.

The good news is that user acquisition is not the mysterious dark art that big tech companies want you to believe it is. They spend millions on advertising because they can, not because they have to. As a solo developer armed with vibe coding tools and a scrappy entrepreneurial mindset, you have advantages that massive corporations can only dream about. You can move fast, pivot instantly, engage authentically, and exploit opportunities that would take a Fortune 500 company six months of committee meetings to even acknowledge. The playing field has never been more level, and this chapter is your playbook for winning the user acquisition game without emptying your bank account in the process.

The Art Of Selling, But Also Marketing

Let us start with the foundation of free organic growth, which is App Store Optimization, commonly known as ASO. Think of ASO as search engine optimization for app stores, and understand that most of your competitors are doing it terribly or not at all. When someone searches for a solution to their problem in the App Store or Google Play, the algorithm decides which apps to show them based on a complex cocktail of factors that you can absolutely influence. Your app title is prime real estate, and you need to use it strategically. If you built a meditation app, calling it something clever like ZenMind Pro sounds nice but tells the algorithm nothing. Compare that to Meditation Timer and Sleep Sounds or Daily Calm Meditation for Beginners, which pack in searchable keywords while still sounding legitimate. The difference in discoverability is staggering.

Your app description is another goldmine that most developers treat like an afterthought. The first few lines need to hook potential users immediately because that is all they see before clicking read more, and most people never click. But beyond the hook, you need to naturally incorporate every relevant keyword phrase that someone might search when looking for an app like yours. Do not stuff keywords awkwardly because the algorithms have gotten smarter about that, but do think about the dozens of different ways people might describe what they need. Someone looking for a budget tracker might search expense manager, money planner, spending tracker, financial organizer, or simply budget app. Your description should touch on all these variations while still reading like compelling copy written by a human being who actually cares about helping users.

Screenshots and preview videos might seem like afterthoughts, but they are conversion machines. Studies consistently show that apps with well-designed screenshots and a compelling preview video see dramatically higher download rates, sometimes two to three times higher than those without. You do not need to hire a design agency for this. Tools like Canva, Figma, and even AI image generators can help you create professional looking screenshots that highlight your app's key features and benefits. Show the transformation, not just the interface. If your app helps people track habits, show a screenshot of someone's streak reaching thirty days with celebratory confetti. If your app helps people learn languages, show a progress screen demonstrating mastery. People download apps because they want results, so your screenshots should promise those results visually.

Now let us talk about the guerrilla marketing tactics that can generate your first users without spending a dime on advertising. Reddit is an absolute goldmine for app developers, but you need to approach it correctly or you will get banned into oblivion faster than you can say self promotion. The key is to become a genuine contributing member of communities related to your app's niche long before you ever mention what you have built. If you created a fitness tracking app, spend a few weeks genuinely helping people in fitness subreddits, answering questions, sharing insights, and building karma. Then, when you do mention your app, frame it as a solution you built to solve your own problem, ask for feedback, and be transparent about being the developer. Reddit users have finely tuned spam detectors, but they also love supporting indie developers who approach them authentically.

Product Hunt remains one of the most powerful launch platforms for new apps, and timing your launch correctly can mean the difference between dozens of users and thousands. Launch on Tuesday, Wednesday, or Thursday when traffic is highest. Prepare your Product Hunt page meticulously with compelling images, a clear value proposition, and answers ready for the questions that will inevitably come. Rally whatever network you have to upvote and comment early because the algorithm favors products that gain traction in the first few hours. Even if you have no existing audience, you can join maker communities on platforms like X, Discord, and Indie Hackers where developers support each other's launches through mutual engagement.

Speaking of communities, the build in public movement has created an incredibly powerful user acquisition channel that costs nothing but your willingness to be transparent. Document your app development journey on social media, sharing wins, struggles, and lessons learned along the way. This accomplishes several things simultaneously. It builds an audience of people who feel invested in your success before you even launch. It creates content that attracts others facing similar problems. And it establishes you as a real human being rather than a faceless app in the store, which dramatically increases trust and download willingness. Some developers have built audiences of tens of thousands simply by sharing their journey of building apps with vibe coding tools, turning their learning process into a marketing engine.

Content marketing is another weapon in your arsenal that scales beautifully over time. Create blog posts, YouTube videos, or TikTok content that addresses the problems your app solves without directly pitching your app constantly. If you built a recipe organization app, create content about meal planning strategies, reducing food waste, or cooking on a budget. People searching for these topics find your content, see you as an authority, and naturally discover your app as the tool that makes everything easier. This approach requires patience because content marketing is a long game, but the users it generates are often the most valuable because they arrive already trusting you and understanding the problem you solve.

Let us discuss a tactic that most developers completely overlook, which is partnership marketing with micro influencers. When you hear influencer marketing, you probably imagine paying Kim Kardashian a million dollars to hold your app awkwardly while pretending she uses it. Forget that entirely. Instead, identify creators with small but engaged audiences in your niche, people with one thousand to fifty thousand followers who actually interact with their community. Reach out with a genuine pitch offering free lifetime access to your app, perhaps a small payment if you have budget, and a unique promo code to track conversions. Many micro influencers are thrilled to discover products they genuinely like and will promote them with an authenticity that mega influencers cannot match. One viral TikTok from a creator who genuinely loves your app can generate more downloads than thousands of dollars in paid advertising.

Email marketing is old school but devastatingly effective when done right. Before you even launch your app, create a simple landing page describing what you are building and collecting email addresses from interested users. You can build this in hours using vibe coding tools or no-code platforms like Carrd or ConvertKit's landing pages. When launch day arrives, you have a list of people who specifically asked to be notified, which means they are exponentially more likely to download, leave reviews, and spread the word. After launch, continue collecting emails through your app by offering value like tips, updates, or exclusive features in exchange for email signup. This owned audience becomes incredibly valuable for future app launches and updates.

The cross promotion strategy is something larger developers use constantly that solo developers often miss. Once you have one app with users, every subsequent app becomes easier to launch because you can promote new apps to your existing user base. But even with your first app, you can partner with other indie developers to cross promote. Find apps that serve a similar audience but do not directly compete with yours, and propose a mutually beneficial promotion. If you built a journaling app, partner with a meditation app developer to promote each other. Both of you get exposure to pre-qualified audiences at zero cost, and the endorsement from a related app carries more weight than random advertising.

Review and rating optimization deserves serious attention because social proof dramatically affects download decisions and app store rankings. The most important thing to understand is that happy users rarely leave reviews spontaneously, while unhappy users are highly motivated to complain publicly. You need to proactively ask satisfied users for reviews, but timing and approach matter enormously. Request reviews after positive experiences within your app, such as completing a milestone, achieving a goal, or receiving value. Never interrupt users with review requests during critical tasks or immediately after launching the app. Use native review prompts that Apple and Google provide because they allow users to rate without leaving the app, dramatically increasing completion rates. Some developers report tripling their review counts simply by implementing smart review request timing.

Now here is a growth hacking strategy that sounds almost too simple but works remarkably well, which is making your app inherently shareable. Build features that users naturally want to share with others. This could be achievement cards they can post to social media, referral systems that reward both the inviter and invitee, collaborative features that require inviting friends, or simply results so impressive that users want to show them off. The best viral loops feel valuable to users rather than promotional. When someone shares their language learning streak of one hundred days or their fitness transformation tracked in your app, they are expressing pride in their achievement while simultaneously advertising your product to their entire network.

Localization is massively underutilized by indie developers, and it represents relatively low hanging fruit for user acquisition. English speaking markets are the most competitive, with countless apps fighting for attention. But many other languages have hungry users and far less competition. Translating your app and store listing into Spanish, Portuguese, German, French, Japanese, or Korean can open up entirely new markets where your competition is minimal. AI translation tools have become remarkably good, though you should ideally have a native speaker review critical user facing text. Some developers report that localized versions of their apps outperform the original English version simply because they face so much less competition.

Let me address paid advertising briefly, not because you need it to succeed but because knowing when and how to use it strategically can accelerate growth once you have proven product market fit. The cardinal sin of app advertising is spending money before you have optimized your organic conversion funnel. If your app store page only converts two percent of visitors into downloads, paid traffic will bleed money. First optimize your screenshots, description, and overall presentation until organic conversion rates are respectable, then consider spending money to pour more traffic into your now efficient funnel. Start with tiny budgets of five to twenty dollars per day on platforms like Apple Search Ads, Google Ads, or social media platforms. Test multiple ad variations, measure cost per install obsessively, and only scale what works. Many successful app businesses spend nothing on advertising, while others use it strategically to amplify already working organic strategies.

The path to your first thousand users is not a mystery requiring massive budgets or marketing genius. It requires consistent execution of proven strategies, willingness to put yourself out there authentically, and patience to let compound effects build over time. Your first hundred users might come slowly through personal outreach and community engagement. Your next five hundred might accelerate through content marketing and partnerships starting to generate traffic. Your final four hundred might pour in as app store algorithms recognize your improving metrics and boost your visibility. Each stage feels different, but they all require the same fundamental commitment to providing value and making sure the right people know about it.

Remember that every massive app started with zero users just like yours. The developers who succeeded were not necessarily smarter or better funded, they were simply more persistent and strategic about getting their creations in front of people who needed them. You have built something valuable using vibe coding tools that would have been impossible for you to create just a few years ago. Now your job is to make sure that value reaches the people whose lives it can improve, and in doing so, build the income stream you are working toward. The users are out there searching for exactly what you have built. Your mission now is to make sure they find it.

Scale The Empire

Congratulations are in order. You have done what most people only dream about during their morning commute or while mindlessly scrolling through social media. You have built an app. You have shipped it. You have monetized it. And now, somewhere in the world, money is trickling into your bank account while you sleep, eat breakfast, or binge-watch that series everyone keeps recommending. This is the moment where most people would pat themselves on the back, update their LinkedIn headline to include the word entrepreneur, and coast on this single victory for the rest of their days. But you are not most people. You picked up this book because you understand that life-changing income does not come from a single lucky break. It comes from building systems that multiply success. It comes from thinking like an empire builder rather than a lottery winner.

The difference between someone who makes a few hundred dollars from an app and someone who generates genuine wealth is not talent, luck, or even a superior product. It is the mindset shift from creator to architect.

When you built your first app, you were learning the craft, getting your hands dirty, and proving to yourself that this vibe coding thing actually works. Now that you have that proof, your job description changes entirely. You are no longer just the person who builds apps. You are the person who builds systems that build apps. This distinction might sound like semantic gymnastics, but it represents the most important mental leap you will make in your entire app development journey.

Think about it this way. A baker who makes excellent croissants can earn a good living selling them at a single location. But a baker who figures out how to replicate that croissant recipe across multiple locations, train others to execute it perfectly, and systematize the entire operation can build a bakery empire. The croissants might be identical, but the outcomes are wildly different. Your first successful app is your proof-of-concept croissant. It is delicious, it generates revenue, and people seem to like it. Now we need to turn you into the person who opens bakeries, not just the person who wakes up at four in the morning to knead dough.

The beautiful reality of app development in the vibe coding era is that scaling does not require hiring an army of developers or raising venture capital. The same tools that helped you build your first app in hours can help you build your tenth app in even less time because you now understand the process, the prompts, and the patterns that work. Your accumulated knowledge becomes a force multiplier. Every lesson learned from your first app makes your second app better. Every bug you debugged teaches you what to avoid. Every user complaint reveals opportunities you had not considered. This compounding effect is the foundation of scaling, and it starts with recognizing that your experience is now one of your most valuable assets.

Let us talk about automation, because this is where the magic of scaling truly begins. When you had one app, manually checking reviews, responding to user feedback, and monitoring download numbers was manageable. It might have even felt exciting, like watching a garden you planted slowly bloom. But when you have three apps, five apps, or ten apps, this manual approach becomes a full-time job that leaves no time for building new products or enjoying the income you are generating. The solution is not to abandon these important tasks but to create systems that handle them automatically or alert you only when your attention is genuinely required.

Consider the update cycle as your first target for automation. Your apps need regular updates to fix bugs, add features users request, and stay compatible with the latest operating system versions. Instead of approaching each update as a fresh project, create a template workflow that applies to all your apps. This might include a monthly review of user feedback across all products, a quarterly feature prioritization session, and a standardized testing checklist that ensures nothing breaks when you push changes. The vibe coding tools you already know can help here too. You can describe update tasks to your AI assistant in batch form, asking it to generate the code for similar improvements across multiple apps simultaneously. What once took dedicated attention for each product becomes a systematic process you can execute in an afternoon.

Monitoring tools become essential at scale. Services exist that track your app store rankings, notify you of new reviews, alert you to crashes, and compile analytics across multiple applications into single dashboards. Investing time in setting up these monitoring systems pays dividends forever. Instead of manually logging into five different app store accounts to check your numbers, you wake up to a single email or dashboard that tells you everything you need to know. This is not laziness. This is leverage. The entrepreneurs who build empires understand that their attention is a finite resource that must be allocated strategically. Every minute you save through automation is a minute you can invest in building your next income-generating product.

You Can't Do It Alone, Trust Me

Now we arrive at a topic that makes some solo developers uncomfortable: outsourcing. There is a certain pride in saying you built everything yourself, handled every aspect of the business, and never relied on anyone else. This pride is understandable but ultimately limiting. The wealthiest app entrepreneurs recognize that their job is to focus on the activities that generate the most value while delegating everything else to people or tools that can handle it more efficiently. This does not mean abandoning quality control or becoming disconnected from your products. It means recognizing that your time has a value, and spending three hours on a task someone else could do for thirty dollars is actually losing you money.

Start by identifying the tasks in your app business that drain your energy, take excessive time, or require skills that are not your strength. For many vibe coding entrepreneurs, this includes graphic design, customer support, app store optimization research, and marketing content creation. Each of these areas has freelance specialists who can deliver professional results at reasonable prices. Platforms like Fiverr, Upwork, and specialized app development marketplaces connect you with talented people around the world who would love to help your apps succeed. The key is starting small, building relationships with reliable contractors, and gradually expanding your team of trusted collaborators.

Think of outsourcing as building your board of advisors and helpers. You might hire a graphic designer who creates all your app icons and screenshots, ensuring consistent branding across your portfolio. You might engage a virtual assistant who monitors reviews and drafts response templates for your approval. You might work with a marketing specialist who handles your social media presence and ASO optimization. None of these people need to be full-time employees. The gig economy has created a flexible workforce perfectly suited for app entrepreneurs who need high-quality help without traditional employment overhead. Your job becomes directing this team, making strategic decisions, and focusing on the creative work of identifying new opportunities and building new products.

The financial math of outsourcing often surprises people when they actually calculate it. If your time is worth fifty dollars an hour based on the income your apps generate, then any task you can outsource for less than fifty dollars per hour represents a net gain. That customer support hour you delegated for fifteen dollars freed up an hour you could use to build features that generate hundreds of dollars in additional revenue. This is not about being cheap with your contractors. Pay fair rates, treat people well, and build relationships that last. The point is recognizing that strategic delegation multiplies your capacity rather than diminishing your role.

Build Up Your Empire Porfolio

The question of how many apps to run simultaneously deserves careful consideration. There is no magic number that applies to everyone because it depends on your available time, the complexity of your applications, and your personal capacity for context switching. However, most successful app portfolio owners find that three to five actively maintained apps represents a sweet spot. This number allows for meaningful diversification without spreading yourself so thin that quality suffers. Each app in your portfolio should receive enough attention to maintain its revenue and growth trajectory. If you find yourself neglecting apps to the point where reviews go unanswered for weeks and bugs persist for months, you have exceeded your current capacity.

The portfolio approach to app development offers several advantages beyond simple revenue multiplication. Risk diversification means that if one app experiences a sudden drop in downloads due to algorithm changes or new competition, your other apps continue generating income. Different apps often have complementary seasonal patterns, with some performing better during holidays while others peak during back-to-school season or summer months. Portfolio ownership also allows you to cross-promote between your apps, using the audience of one successful product to bootstrap downloads for a new launch. Users who enjoy one of your apps are pre-qualified as people who might enjoy your other offerings.

Launching multiple apps simultaneously or in rapid succession requires a different approach than your first careful, methodical app development experience. You now have the knowledge to move faster, but speed without systems leads to chaos. Create a launch checklist that captures everything you learned from previous releases. This checklist becomes your launch day protocol, ensuring that you do not forget crucial steps in the excitement of shipping something new. App store optimization should be handled before launch day. Promotional materials should be prepared in advance. Beta testers should have provided feedback. When launch day arrives, your job is simply to push the button and execute the plan you have already created.

Consider developing apps that share underlying architecture or design elements. This is not about creating inferior copycat products but about recognizing efficiencies that come from familiarity. If you build three productivity apps that all use similar navigation patterns, database structures, and design systems, you can develop them faster and maintain them more easily. Your vibe coding prompts for common features become refined templates you can adapt for each new project. The AI assistants you work with perform better when you can reference previous successful implementations. This is the software development equivalent of a restaurant chain that uses the same kitchen equipment and training materials across all locations.

Revenue targets help maintain focus as your portfolio grows. Set specific monthly or quarterly income goals for your app business and track progress toward them. These targets create accountability and help you make decisions about where to invest your limited time and resources. If one app is dramatically outperforming others, it might deserve additional features and marketing attention. If another app consistently underperforms despite your efforts, it might be time to sunset it and redirect that energy toward a new opportunity. Data-driven decision making becomes increasingly important as your portfolio grows because gut feelings become unreliable when you are managing multiple products across different niches.

The concept of app business systems deserves its own consideration. A system is a repeatable process that produces consistent results. Your app business should eventually run on systems for everything from idea validation to launch to maintenance to eventual retirement.

Document your processes as you develop them. When you discover an effective way to handle customer support inquiries, write it down. When you figure out the optimal schedule for app updates, document it. When you identify the most effective keywords for app store optimization in your niche, record them. This documentation serves two purposes. First, it ensures you do not forget hard-won lessons. Second, it allows you to eventually delegate these tasks to others because you have created training materials without even trying.

The psychological shift from hustle to empire building requires abandoning some habits that served you well initially. Answering every email immediately, personally handling every customer interaction, and manually optimizing every detail were appropriate when you had one app and all the time in the world. These behaviors become bottlenecks at scale. Your new job is building systems that handle these tasks without your direct involvement. This transition feels uncomfortable at first because it seems like you are losing control. In reality, you are gaining leverage. The app entrepreneur who successfully scales learns to measure success not by how busy they are but by how much income the business generates relative to the time invested.

Building an app empire through vibe coding represents a genuine opportunity that did not exist even a few years ago. The technical barriers that once required teams of developers and significant capital have been obliterated by AI-powered tools that turn your ideas into functional products. The distribution barriers that once required publisher relationships and marketing budgets have been democratized through app stores that give anyone access to billions of potential users. What remains is the entrepreneurial challenge of building systems, making smart decisions, and executing consistently over time. These challenges are substantial, but they are not technical. They are not gatekept by credentials or access. They are simply the work of building a business, and now you have the tools to do exactly that.

Your journey from first app to app empire will not happen overnight, and it should not. Each app you launch teaches you something new about markets, users, and yourself. Each challenge you overcome adds to your entrepreneurial education. Each success builds the confidence and resources needed for bigger ambitions. The blueprint you now possess is not a guarantee of wealth but a map showing a path that others have walked successfully. Your job is to walk that path, adapt it to your circumstances, and ultimately create your own version of app business success. The empire awaits. It is time to start building.

50 App Ideas You Can Use Now

Welcome to the goldmine chapter, the one you'll probably bookmark, screenshot, and return to every time you're sitting at your laptop wondering what to build next. By now you understand the power of vibe coding, you've learned how to communicate with AI effectively, and you know how to debug common issues. What you need now is inspiration, and not just any inspiration but concrete, actionable ideas that real people actually want to pay for. This chapter delivers exactly that. Fifty app ideas across ten different categories, each one carefully selected because it solves a genuine problem, has proven market demand, and most importantly can be built by someone exactly like you using nothing but natural language prompts and the platforms you've already learned about.

Let me be clear about something before we dive in. These aren't theoretical concepts dreamed up in some ivory tower. These are practical applications based on market research, app store trends, and the actual pain points real humans experience every single day. Some of these ideas are deliberately simple because sometimes the most profitable apps are embarrassingly straightforward. Others have more complexity because the market rewards comprehensive solutions in certain niches. The key is matching your skill level and ambition with the right opportunity.

Each category includes five detailed app concepts, example prompts you can use immediately or adapt to your vision, and careful considerations specific to that category that could make or break your success. Think of this chapter as your personal idea vault, one you can raid whenever entrepreneurial inspiration runs dry. Let's get into it.

Productivity & Utility Apps

The Productivity and Utility space represents the bread and butter of app development for a reason. These apps solve boring problems, and boring problems are beautiful because they happen to everyone, they happen frequently, and people will gladly pay to make them disappear. The vibe here is sleek and fast, which means your app needs to do one thing exceptionally well rather than fifty things adequately.

The first idea in this category is a **Meeting Cost Calculator**, an app that runs during meetings and displays in real time how much money the meeting is costing based on the salaries of attendees. This sounds almost comical until you realize that corporate professionals are obsessed with productivity metrics and managers love tools that help justify their decisions. The app would let users input participant salary ranges or use industry averages, then display a running dollar counter as the meeting progresses. You could create this by prompting something like:

"Build a mobile app with a clean professional interface that calculates meeting costs in real time. Users should be able to add participants with their hourly rates or select from preset salary ranges.

Include a start and stop button that runs a timer and displays the cumulative cost as the meeting progresses. Add a history feature that saves past meetings with their total costs and durations. Make it look sleek and corporate with a dark blue and white color scheme."

The monetization path here is clear with a free version allowing three meetings per week and a premium tier for unlimited tracking plus exportable reports that managers can use in presentations.

The second productivity idea is a **Screenshot Organizer** that uses AI to automatically categorize and make searchable all the screenshots cluttering up your camera roll. Everyone takes screenshots constantly but finding that one image of that one thing from three months ago feels like archaeological excavation. This app would scan screenshot text using optical character recognition and apply smart tags while allowing users to search with natural language queries. Your prompt could be:

"Create an app that helps users organize their screenshots. The app should request access to the photo library and scan only images that appear to be screenshots or are saved in a screenshot folder. Use OCR to extract any text from screenshots and allow users to search their collection using natural language. Include automatic category

suggestions like receipts, conversations, social media, and instructions. Design a grid view gallery with a prominent search bar and create a clean minimal interface in light mode with a white and soft gray palette."

Consider that this app handles sensitive data since screenshots often contain private conversations, passwords, and personal information, which means you need to process everything locally on the device rather than sending images to external servers.

Third is a **Voice Memo Summarizer** that records audio and provides AI-generated summaries, action items, and searchable transcripts. The difference between this and basic voice recording apps is intelligence. People record meetings, lectures, ideas, and conversations but rarely have time to listen back to forty-five-minute recordings. This app does the heavy lifting. Prompt with:

"Build a voice recording app that creates AI-powered summaries. Include a large prominent record button, a list view of past recordings, and playback functionality. After recording, use AI to generate a written transcript, a three-sentence summary, and a bullet list of action items or key points. Allow users to search across all their

recordings by keyword. Use a warm professional color scheme with orange accents on a cream background."

The key consideration here is transcript accuracy which varies dramatically based on audio quality, accents, and background noise, so you need to set appropriate user expectations and potentially offer manual editing of transcripts.

Fourth in productivity is a **Subscription Tracker** that monitors all recurring charges and alerts users before renewals while calculating their total monthly subscription burden. The average American has more subscriptions than they realize and regularly gets charged for services they've forgotten about. This app creates awareness and saves money which users deeply appreciate. Your prompt might read:

"Create a subscription tracking app where users can manually add their recurring subscriptions or connect their email to auto-detect subscription receipts. Display the total monthly and yearly cost prominently at the top. Send push notifications three days before any subscription renews. Include a category breakdown showing how much users spend on streaming, software, fitness, and other categories. Use a minimalist design with green accents representing money savings."

Note that if you implement email scanning for auto-detection, you're handling extremely sensitive data and need robust privacy policies plus secure handling practices.

The fifth productivity app idea is a **Clipboard Manager** that saves everything users copy and lets them search, organize, and access their copy history across multiple days or weeks. This seems trivial until you realize how often people copy something, switch apps, copy something else, and lose the first item forever. A persistent searchable clipboard history eliminates this frustration entirely. Prompt with:

"Build a clipboard manager app that runs in the background and saves everything the user copies. Create a chronological list view of copied items with the most recent at top. Allow searching through clipboard history. Let users star important items to pin them to a favorites section. Include an option to organize items into custom folders. Design with a neutral gray and white interface that feels like a system utility rather than a flashy consumer app."

The consideration here is battery life and privacy since an app constantly monitoring the clipboard needs to be extremely efficient and must clearly communicate to users what data is being stored.

Finance & Fintech

Moving into Finance and Fintech, we enter territory where trust is everything. Users will abandon even a brilliant finance app instantly if it feels sketchy, unprofessional, or insecure. The vibe here is secure, trustworthy, and data-heavy but presented simply. Never sacrifice clarity for cleverness in this category.

The first finance idea is an **Envelope Budgeting** App based on the classic cash envelope system but digitized. Users allocate money into virtual envelopes for different spending categories and the app tracks spending against each envelope in real time. When an envelope runs empty, that category is done for the month. Prompt this with:

"Create a budgeting app based on the envelope method. Users should be able to create custom envelope categories like groceries, entertainment, and transportation. They set a monthly budget for each envelope and then log expenses that deduct from the appropriate envelope. Display remaining amounts with visual progress bars that turn from green to yellow to red as envelopes empty. Include a monthly reset feature and historical spending reports. Use a calm trustworthy color palette with navy blue and white."

For finance apps, consider that users may want to sync data across devices, which requires cloud storage and authentication, and they may be extremely sensitive about who can potentially access their financial information.

Second is a **Tip Calculator and Bill Splitter** specifically designed for groups at restaurants with support for unequal splits, separate items, and tip adjustments. Yes, tip calculators exist, but most are clunky and none handle the complex reality of six people at dinner where two people shared an appetizer, one person only had a salad, and everyone wants to tip differently. Your prompt should be:

"Build a bill splitting app for groups at restaurants. Users enter the total bill, add the names of people splitting it, and then can either split equally or assign specific dollar amounts to each person. Include tip calculation with preset percentages and custom input. Handle tax distribution automatically. Add a feature where users can photograph a receipt and manually assign each line item to different people. Use a friendly approachable design with rounded buttons and a warm color scheme of coral and cream."

The major consideration is accuracy because a bug that costs someone even fifty cents will generate immediate one-star reviews. Test your math thoroughly.

Third is a **No-Spend Day Tracker**, a gamified savings app that challenges users to have as many days as possible without spending money. This taps into the psychology of streaks and the satisfaction of self-discipline. Users mark each day as a spend or no-spend day and compete against their own past performance or friends. Prompt with:

"Create a minimalist savings challenge app focused on no-spend days. Display a calendar view where users tap each day to mark it green for no spending or red for spending. Track current streak, longest streak, and monthly ratio of no-spend days. Include motivational messages that appear when users extend their streak. Allow optional connection to friends to share and compare streaks without revealing actual financial information. Design with a clean nature-inspired aesthetic using white backgrounds with green leaf accents."

The gamification must feel encouraging rather than punishing because shaming users for spending money backfires and causes app abandonment.

Fourth is a **Spare Change Roundup Visualizer** that doesn't actually move money but shows users how much they would save if they rounded up every purchase to the nearest dollar. Actual round-up investing apps require serious regulatory compliance, but a simulator that helps users understand the concept and plan their savings requires no financial licenses. Your prompt could be:

"Build an educational app that simulates spare change saving. Users manually enter their purchases or connect to view notifications of spending, then the app calculates what the round-up amount would be for each transaction. Display a growing virtual jar that fills with these hypothetical savings. Show projected yearly savings based on spending patterns. Include educational content about how actual roundup investing works. Use a piggy bank theme with soft pink and gold colors in a friendly approachable design."

The critical consideration is making absolutely clear that this app does not move real money and is for educational and planning purposes only.

Fifth in finance is an **Invoice Generator for Freelancers** that creates professional PDF invoices from simple inputs. Freelancers hate administrative work and will pay for tools that make it painless. This app should turn minimal information into polished documents clients actually respect. Prompt this with:

"Create an invoice generation app for freelancers. Users create a profile with their business name, address, and payment details. They can then quickly generate invoices by entering client information, line items with descriptions and amounts, and due dates. Generate a professional PDF invoice that can be emailed directly from the app or downloaded. Include automatic invoice numbering, payment tracking, and reminders for overdue invoices. Design with a corporate professional aesthetic using charcoal gray and white with subtle blue accents."

Remember that invoices are legal documents, so ensure proper formatting, tax calculations if applicable, and clear terms. Research invoicing requirements for major markets.

Health & Fitness

Health and Fitness apps live or die on motivation. Users download these apps with the best intentions, then abandon them within weeks. The vibe needs to be either high energy and motivational or deeply calming for mental health applications. Your design choices should actively support the emotional state you want to create.

The first health idea is a **Water Intake Tracker** with customized reminders based on activity level, weather, and personal hydration goals. Drinking enough water is a universal struggle and people genuinely forget. An app that nudges them intelligently rather than annoyingly can become part of their daily routine. Prompt with:

"Build a water tracking app with smart reminders. Users set their daily hydration goal based on weight and activity level. They log water intake by tapping preset cup sizes or custom amounts. The app sends customizable interval reminders that pause during typical sleep hours. Include a daily progress ring visualization and weekly hydration trends. Add achievement badges for streak milestones. Use a fresh clean aesthetic with light blue gradients and water droplet imagery."

The consideration here is notification fatigue. Too many reminders and users disable them entirely, too few and the app provides no value. Let users customize reminder frequency and timing.

Second is a **Stretching Routine App** focused specifically on desk workers and remote employees who sit all day. This isn't a generic exercise app but a specialized tool for people whose bodies suffer from computer work. Short targeted routines make this realistic to actually use during work breaks. Your prompt should be:

"Create a stretching app designed for people who work at desks. Include curated five-minute and ten-minute stretching routines targeting neck, shoulders, back, wrists, and hip flexors. Each stretch should have a clear illustration or animation, written instructions, and a countdown timer. Allow users to set break reminders throughout their workday. Track weekly stretching consistency with a simple visual. Use a calm energizing design with teal and white colors and smooth animations that demonstrate each stretch."

Consider that incorrect stretching can cause injury, so include appropriate disclaimers and source movements from verified physical therapy resources.

Third is a **Meal Prep Planner** that helps users plan a week of meals, generates grocery lists automatically, and scales recipes based on how many portions they need. The meal prep community is enormous and dedicated, yet the tools available are surprisingly mediocre. Your prompt could be:

"Build a meal planning app focused on weekly meal prep. Include a library of meal prep friendly recipes that users can browse by cuisine, cooking time, and dietary preference. Users drag recipes onto a weekly calendar and the app generates a consolidated grocery list that combines ingredients intelligently. Allow recipe scaling based on desired portions. Include storage and reheating instructions for each meal. Design with a warm inviting food-focused aesthetic using terracotta and cream colors with large appealing food imagery."

The main consideration is that recipe content requires either original creation, proper licensing, or user-generated contributions. Never copy recipes from other sources without permission.

Fourth is a **Medication Reminder App** that ensures users never forget a dose and tracks adherence over time for discussion with healthcare providers. This serves an older demographic and those with chronic conditions who take multiple medications. Reliability is absolutely critical here because missed medications can have serious health consequences. Prompt with:

"Create a medication reminder app with serious reliability. Users add their medications with name, dosage, frequency, and timing. The app sends push notifications at exact scheduled times with confirmation buttons for taking or skipping doses. Include a calendar view showing medication adherence history and the ability to export reports as PDF for doctor visits. Add features for tracking refill dates and pharmacy information. Design with large easily readable text, high contrast colors for accessibility, and a simple trustworthy medical aesthetic using white and soft blue."

The critical consideration is that this app has real health implications. Test notification reliability obsessively, include failsafes, and avoid any features that could be misinterpreted as medical advice.

Fifth in health is a **Symptom Journal** that helps users track physical symptoms over time to identify patterns and communicate more effectively with doctors. Chronic illness sufferers and those with mysterious recurring issues need this data but struggle to remember details during brief medical appointments. Your prompt should be:

"Build a symptom tracking app for health journaling. Users log entries describing symptoms with pain level on a scale, duration,

location on a body diagram, and notes about possible triggers. Include fields for related factors like sleep, stress, weather, and menstrual cycle. Generate visual reports showing symptom frequency and severity over time. Allow exporting summaries for medical appointments. Use a neutral calming design with lavender and white, ensuring the app feels supportive rather than clinical."

Remember that anything resembling diagnosis or treatment suggestion is firmly in regulated medical device territory, so this must remain purely a tracking and journaling tool.

Lifestyle

Lifestyle apps are where aesthetics matter most because people use these apps to curate and beautify their lives, meaning the app itself must be beautiful. The vibe is highly personal, so customization options can be a major differentiator. These apps often become part of someone's daily ritual rather than a tool they use occasionally.

The first lifestyle idea is a **Digital Wardrobe Organizer** where users photograph their clothing and the app helps them plan outfits, track what they haven't worn recently, and potentially suggest combinations. People buy clothes they forget about and recreate the same boring outfits out of habit. This app breaks that pattern. Prompt with:

"Create a wardrobe management app where users photograph their clothing items. Include category organization for tops, bottoms, dresses, shoes, and accessories. Users can create outfit combinations by selecting pieces that are then displayed together. Track wear frequency and flag items that haven't been worn in months with suggestions to donate or style differently. Include a calendar view for planning outfits in advance. Design with a luxurious fashion-forward aesthetic using black, white, and gold with elegant typography."

Consider that photo quality dramatically affects user experience, so provide guidance on photographing clothes effectively or include basic image editing tools.

Second is a **Plant Care Companion** that sends watering and care reminders customized to each specific plant species, lighting conditions, and season. Plant parenthood is a massive trend and plant death is a massive problem. People want help keeping their green friends alive. Your prompt could be:

"Build a plant care app that helps users keep their houseplants healthy. Users add plants by species with a searchable database of common houseplants including care requirements. The app generates customized watering and care schedules based on plant type, light conditions, and season. Send smart reminders that account for environmental factors. Include a journal feature for tracking plant growth with photos over time. Design with a natural organic aesthetic using sage green and cream with botanical illustrations."

The care advice must be botanically accurate since incorrect watering schedules kill plants, so source information from horticultural databases and include appropriate disclaimers.

Third is a **Morning Routine Builder** that helps users design and execute their ideal morning routine with timed segments and a guided flow. Productivity enthusiasts obsess over morning routines but struggle with consistency and timing. This app turns their ideal routine into a guided experience. Prompt with:

"Create a morning routine app that guides users through their customized morning ritual. Users build their routine by adding timed segments like meditation for ten minutes, journaling for five minutes, and exercise for twenty minutes. When activated, the app moves through each segment with timers, optional ambient sounds, and transitions between activities. Track routine completion streaks and show analytics on which segments get skipped most often. Design with a sunrise-inspired gradient aesthetic using soft oranges and pinks with calming sans-serif typography."

Consider that this app must respect the user's pace, so include easy pause and skip functions rather than creating stress about keeping up.

Fourth is an **Interior Design Color Palette Generator** that uses camera input to analyze a room and suggest complementary color schemes for redecorating. Home decorating is intimidating because people fear making expensive color mistakes. This tool provides professional-quality guidance to normal homeowners. Your prompt should be:

"Build an interior design app that helps users choose color palettes. Users photograph a room and the app identifies existing colors in furniture, flooring, and fixtures. It then generates complementary color palette suggestions for walls, accents, and decor. Include the ability to save favorite palettes and see example rooms using similar color schemes. Provide paint color matches from major brands if possible. Design with a sophisticated minimalist aesthetic using neutral grays and whites with colorful swatches as the primary visual interest."

Color accuracy depends heavily on photo lighting conditions, so include guidance on taking representative photos and provide multiple palette options to account for variation.

Fifth in lifestyle is a **Gratitude Journal** with Prompts that provides daily journaling prompts, streak tracking, and the ability to look back on past entries. Gratitude journaling has proven mental health benefits, but staring at a blank page is intimidating. Prompts remove the barrier and encourage deeper reflection. Prompt with:

"Create a gratitude journaling app with daily prompts. Each day presents a unique prompt for reflection such as 'What small moment brought you joy today?' or 'Who made your day better and how?' Users write entries that are saved with the date and prompt. Include a streak tracker for daily journaling consistency and a lookback feature that resurfaces entries from the same date in previous years. Design with a warm cozy aesthetic using soft beige and burnt orange with handwriting-style fonts for a personal touch."

The consideration is that prompts must be thoughtfully written and diverse enough that users don't see obvious repetition within their first few months of use.

Education (EdTech)

Education apps succeed when they make learning feel like achievement rather than work. The vibe is engaging, gamified, and structured, meaning progress must be visible and accomplishments must feel rewarding. Users should end each session feeling smarter, not frustrated.

The first EdTech idea is a **Typing Speed Trainer** designed specifically for mobile keyboards, helping users improve their smartphone typing speed and accuracy through timed exercises. We obsess over desktop typing skills but spend most of our time typing on phones where most people are surprisingly slow. This is an untapped niche with real utility. Prompt with:

"Build a typing practice app for improving mobile keyboard speed. Include various exercise types such as typing prompted sentences, copying displayed text accurately, and timed speed tests. Track words per minute and accuracy over time with visual progress graphs. Add different content categories like quotes, business email phrases, and casual conversation. Include leaderboards for competitive users. Design with an energetic modern aesthetic using bright blue and white with satisfying animations for achievements."

Consider that different phone sizes and keyboard apps affect results, so focus on improvement over absolute metrics and avoid comparing users on different devices directly.

Second is a **Language Phrase Book** focused on practical travel phrases for a specific language with audio pronunciation, spaced repetition, and category organization. Unlike comprehensive language learning apps, this targets travelers who need functional communication quickly rather than fluency. Your prompt could be:

"Create a travel phrase book app for learning practical phrases in Spanish. Organize phrases into categories like greetings, ordering food, transportation, emergencies, and shopping. Include audio pronunciation for each phrase, phonetic spelling, and the ability to favorite frequently needed phrases for quick access. Implement spaced repetition for learning with daily practice reminders. Design with a travel-inspired aesthetic using passport-blue and warm neutrals with flag iconography."

The key consideration is audio quality and pronunciation accuracy, which must be native speaker level.

Poor pronunciation guidance is worse than no guidance at all.

Third is a **Historical Events Daily** App that teaches one interesting historical event each day with engaging storytelling and optional deep dives. People love learning in small digestible pieces, and history is full of fascinating stories that school somehow made boring. Your prompt should be:

"Build a daily history learning app that presents one interesting historical event each day. Write or curate engaging short-form content that tells each event as a story rather than dry facts. Include the date, key figures involved, and why it matters. Allow users to mark favorites, take a short quiz after reading, and explore related events. Track a learning streak for daily engagement. Design with a sophisticated literary aesthetic using sepia tones and classic serif typography that evokes old books and historical documents."

Content creation is the biggest challenge here since you need three hundred sixty-five unique, well-researched, engaging historical pieces at minimum. Consider starting with a smaller scope or partnering with history content creators.

Fourth is a **Public Speaking Practice** App that records users giving impromptu speeches on random topics, provides timing feedback, and allows playback for self-review. Fear of public speaking is nearly universal, and practice is the only cure. Most people never practice because there's no structure or accountability. Prompt with:

"Create a public speaking practice app that helps users improve their impromptu speaking skills. Generate random speaking prompts across categories like business, opinion, storytelling, and persuasion. Set a timer for one to five minutes and record the user's speech. After recording, provide feedback on duration, filler word detection if possible, and speaking pace. Allow users to save recordings for later review or delete them immediately. Include achievement tracking for speeches completed. Design with a confident professional aesthetic using deep purple and gold that makes users feel like they're stepping onto a stage."

Privacy is crucial here since people are recording themselves potentially at their most vulnerable, so ensure recordings never leave the device unless explicitly exported by the user.

Fifth in education is a **Flashcard Builder with AI Generation** that lets users create study flashcards from any text they input, using AI to automatically generate question and answer pairs. Manual flashcard creation is tedious, which prevents people from using this proven study method. AI removes that barrier. Your prompt could be

"Build a flashcard study app with AI-powered card generation. Users can paste text from textbooks, articles, or notes, and the app uses AI to automatically generate relevant question and answer flashcards. Allow manual card creation and editing as well. Implement spaced repetition scheduling that prioritizes cards the user struggles with. Include study session modes with progress tracking. Design with a clean studious aesthetic using a bright white background with colorful subject-based category tabs."

The AI card generation must be clearly valuable, meaning cards should ask meaningful questions rather than trivial details, so prompt engineering for this feature requires careful attention.

Social Networking & Connection

Social networking apps must create community, which is harder than it sounds. The vibe is community-centric and interactive, meaning users need to feel like they belong to something larger than themselves. Empty social networks are depressing, so you need a plan for bootstrapping initial activity.

The first social idea is a **Book Club Organizer** for finding or forming local book clubs, coordinating reads, scheduling meetings, and facilitating discussions. Reading is fundamentally a solitary activity that people want to make social, and the logistics of book clubs are annoying enough that many never happen. Your prompt should be:

"Create a book club organization app that connects readers. Users create profiles with reading preferences and location. They can browse existing local book clubs or create their own. Each club has a shared calendar for meetings, a current and past books list, and a discussion forum. Include reading progress tracking that club members can optionally share. Send reminders for upcoming meetings and reading milestones. Design with a warm literary aesthetic using rich burgundy and cream with bookshelf imagery."

The cold start problem is severe here, so consider launching in a specific geographic area or partnering with libraries and bookstores rather than trying to serve everywhere initially.

Second is a **Dog Walker Meetup** App for connecting dog owners who walk at similar times and locations so they can arrange joint walks and their dogs can socialize. Dog owners already talk to each other constantly during walks, so this formalizes and facilitates natural behavior. Prompt with:

"Build a dog owner connection app focused on coordinating dog walks. Users create profiles for themselves and their dogs including breed, size, temperament, and favorite walking times and locations. The app suggests nearby compatible dog walking partners based on timing and dog compatibility. Include messaging to arrange meetups and a check-in feature for when walking together. Design with a playful friendly aesthetic using golden yellow and sky blue with cute dog illustrations."

Safety considerations are significant since you're facilitating in-person meetups between strangers. Include profile verification options, public meeting location recommendations, and the ability to report problematic users.

Third is a **Neighborhood Skill Swap Platform** where community members offer and request skill-based favors such as help with moving, tech support, language tutoring, or garden work. This builds community while helping people who can't afford professional services. Your prompt could be:

"Create a neighborhood skill exchange app where users post skills they can offer and help they need. Users list things they're good at and can help neighbors with. They also post requests for help they need. A matching system suggests possible exchanges where both parties benefit. Include a simple reputation system with thank-you reviews. Keep everything hyperlocal by filtering to a specific radius. Design with a welcoming community-focused aesthetic using warm orange and cream with friendly human illustrations."

Hyperlocal apps need density to work, so launching in a single apartment complex or neighborhood first before expanding is essential. Additionally, consider liability when people offer services to each other.

Fourth is a **Hobby Group Finder** that helps people discover local groups for their niche interests, from amateur astronomy to historical European martial arts to competitive Scrabble. Finding other enthusiasts for obscure hobbies is difficult, and loneliness among hobbyists is common. Your prompt should be:

"Build an app for discovering local hobby groups. Users select from a comprehensive list of hobbies and interests. The app shows existing groups in their area or lets them create new ones. Each group has a description, meeting schedule, and member list. Include messaging and event coordination features. Allow private groups for those who want to vet members. Design with a vibrant colorful aesthetic where each hobby category has its own color identity, creating a rainbow of interests on the discovery screen."

Content moderation becomes necessary as the platform grows since some groups may engage in activities you don't want associated with your app, so plan for reporting and removal processes.

Fifth in social is a **Creative Accountability Partner Matcher** that connects writers, artists, musicians, and other creatives with accountability partners who share similar goals for mutual motivation. Creative pursuits are lonely and the dropout rate is enormous. Having someone who expects to hear about your progress dramatically increases follow-through. Prompt with:

"Create an accountability partner app for creative people. Users indicate their creative discipline, current projects, and how much time they want to dedicate weekly. The app matches them with compatible accountability partners based on similar disciplines and schedules. Include a shared progress log where both partners track their work sessions. Add weekly check-in prompts that encourage partners to celebrate wins and troubleshoot challenges. Design with an inspiring artistic aesthetic using deep teal and copper with abstract creative brush stroke elements."

Matching quality determines whether this app creates value, so invest in the matching algorithm and allow users to request new partners if matches don't work out.

Entertainment & Media

Entertainment and Media apps need to be fun first and functional second. The vibe is flashy and highly visual because users come to these apps to enjoy themselves. Performance matters enormously since lag or stuttering kills the entertainment experience instantly.

The first entertainment idea is a **Random Movie Picker** that ends the eternal Netflix scroll by asking a few preference questions and then making a definitive recommendation that users can immediately stream. Analysis paralysis around what to watch wastes millions of hours of human life daily. This app makes the decision so you don't have to. Your prompt should be:

"Create a movie recommendation app that decisively picks what to watch. Users answer three quick questions about their current mood, how much time they have, and one genre they want to avoid. The app then displays one perfect movie recommendation with poster, description, and where it's available to stream. Users can accept the pick or request another with one tap. Include a watched list and the ability to rate recommendations to improve future suggestions. Design with a cinematic aesthetic using deep black and vibrant red with dramatic movie poster styling."

Streaming availability data is challenging to maintain since it changes constantly, so consider whether to include this feature or focus purely on the recommendation.

Second is a **GIF Story Creator** that lets users create short animated stories or messages by arranging GIFs in sequence with text overlays and music. GIFs are everywhere but the tools for creative GIF composition are limited. This enables new forms of expression. Prompt with:

"Build a creative tool for making GIF stories. Users search a GIF database to select multiple GIFs and arrange them in sequence. Add text overlays to each GIF frame with customizable fonts and colors. Optionally add background music from a library of licensed tracks. Preview the complete story and export it as a video file that can be shared anywhere. Design with a playful maximalist aesthetic using rainbow gradients and bold typography that encourages creativity."

GIF licensing is complicated since most GIF databases have usage restrictions, so ensure your implementation respects the terms of whichever GIF API you integrate.

Third is a **Meme Generator with AI Captions** that suggests relevant humorous text for popular meme templates. Making memes is harder than it looks because the format is easy but the comedy timing is difficult. AI can help people be funnier. Your prompt could be:

"Create a meme generation app with AI caption suggestions. Include a library of popular meme templates with clear descriptions of their typical usage context. Users select a template and either write their own caption or ask the AI for suggestions based on a topic or theme they provide. Generate multiple AI caption options to choose from. Include editing tools for text position, font size, and basic image adjustments. Allow direct sharing to social platforms. Design with an irreverent internet-culture aesthetic using chaotic fonts and a deliberately slightly ugly color scheme that fits meme culture."

Meme templates often involve copyrighted images, so research the legal status of each template and err on the side of using only truly public formats.

Fourth is a **Voice Changer with Effects** for recording voice messages with fun filters like chipmunk, robot, demon, or echo, primarily for entertainment and social sharing. Voice filters are endlessly entertaining and the technology is now accessible. This is a straightforward fun app that people actually use. Your prompt should be

"Build a voice recording app with entertaining audio effects. Include a simple record button and a library of voice filters including pitch shift higher, pitch shift lower, robotic processing, echo and reverb, and whisper effect. Users record audio, preview with different effects, and save or share their creations. Include a recent recordings gallery. Design with a fun energetic aesthetic using electric purple and neon green with soundwave visualizations."

Audio processing must happen in real time or near-real time to feel responsive, so optimize for performance and test on older devices.

Fifth in entertainment is a **Daily Wallpaper App** that automatically updates phone wallpaper with beautiful curated images based on user preferences for style, color, and subject matter. Phone wallpapers are personal expression and people love fresh visuals but rarely take time to search for them. Automation solves this perfectly. Prompt with:

"Create a wallpaper app that automatically updates phone backgrounds daily. Users select their preferences for style like nature, abstract, minimal, or artistic, and color preferences. Each day the app selects a wallpaper matching their tastes and updates their phone automatically. Include a gallery of recent wallpapers and the ability to

favorite and return to past images. Allow manual wallpaper exploration and selection as well. Design with a showcase aesthetic where wallpapers are the star, using a dark interface that makes images pop."

Image licensing is critical since you cannot use copyrighted photography without licenses. Either create original images, use properly licensed stock, or integrate with free-use image sources that provide commercial rights.

E-commerce & Marketplaces

E-commerce and Marketplace apps are about trust and transactions. The vibe is clean and organized because users need to feel confident that their money is going to the right place for the right thing. Transaction handling adds significant complexity, so consider whether payment integration is necessary for your minimum viable product.

The first e-commerce idea is a **Local Vintage Marketplace** specifically for buying and selling vintage and antique items within a local area, emphasizing meet-up transactions for items that are impractical to ship. General marketplaces like Facebook Marketplace and Craigslist are chaotic. A curated vintage-focused platform attracts serious collectors. Your prompt should be:

"Build a local marketplace app specifically for vintage and antique items. Sellers create listings with multiple photos, descriptions, era or decade, condition, and price. Include category filtering for furniture, clothing, decor, electronics, and collectibles. Buyers browse local listings and message sellers to arrange meetups. Include a reputation system with reviews after transactions. Design with a nostalgic aesthetic using sepia tones and vintage typography that reflects the content being sold."

Local transactions come with safety considerations, so provide guidance on public meetup locations and consider an optional identity verification feature.

Second is a **Handmade Goods Store Builder** that helps crafters create their own branded app store for their handmade products, separate from larger platforms. Etsy takes significant fees and crafters want direct relationships with customers. A simple personal store app achieves this. Prompt with:

"Create an app builder that lets crafters set up their own product store. Include easy product listing with photos, descriptions, variants, and prices. Integrate basic inventory management to track stock. Implement shopping cart and checkout with payment processing. Allow customization of store appearance including logo, colors, and banner image. Include order management and customer communication features. Design the builder interface with a crafty handmade aesthetic while allowing the resulting stores to reflect each seller's unique brand."

Payment processing integration adds significant complexity and legal requirements, so consider starting with payment instructions rather than actual processing, allowing sellers to accept payment through their preferred existing methods.

Third is a **Service Provider Directory and Booking** for a specific vertical like pet groomers, house cleaners, or personal trainers in a defined geographic area. Generic service directories are overwhelming. Focused verticals can provide much better curation and user experience. Your prompt could be:

"Build a local service directory app for dog groomers in the Los Angeles area. Include business profiles with services offered, pricing, photos of past work, hours, and location. Allow customers to browse by location, filter by specific services, and read reviews. Implement a booking request system where customers propose appointment times and businesses confirm. Include favorites and booking history for customers. Design with a clean professional aesthetic using warm gray and coral that feels premium but approachable."

Launching a local directory requires relationship building with service providers in the area to populate the platform before customers will find it useful.

Fourth is a **Sneaker Collection Manager and Trading Platform** for sneakerheads to catalog their collections, track values, and potentially trade with other collectors. The sneaker collector market is enormous and passionate, with dedicated communities hungry for better tools. Prompt with:

"Create a sneaker collection management app. Users add sneakers from a database of popular releases with photos, release dates, and market values. Track personal collections with purchase price, condition, and storage location. Show estimated current value and total collection worth. Include a trading section where collectors can list sneakers they want to trade and browse what others have available. Design with a streetwear-inspired aesthetic using bold black and white with accent colors that match popular sneaker brand palettes."

Sneaker values fluctuate and users will complain if your pricing data is inaccurate, so either source from reliable APIs or clearly indicate that values are estimates.

Fifth in e-commerce is a **Subscription Box Curation Tool** for small businesses wanting to start subscription box services, helping them manage subscribers, boxes, and shipments. Subscription boxes are a booming business model but the logistics are complex. This tool simplifies operations for small box businesses. Your prompt should be:

"Build a management app for small subscription box businesses. Include subscriber management with payment status, address, and preferences. Create box planning features where owners design upcoming boxes with product lists and quantities needed. Generate packing lists and shipping labels. Track shipments and customer satisfaction. Design with a clean efficient business aesthetic using deep blue and white with clear data visualization for subscriber metrics."

Subscription billing is legally complex with regulations around cancellation, refunds, and renewal notifications, so research requirements thoroughly and consider integrating with established subscription payment platforms rather than building from scratch.

Travel & Local

Travel and Local apps combine adventure with information. The vibe is informative and map-heavy, and the best apps in this category make users feel like they have local knowledge even in unfamiliar places. Offline functionality is often essential since travelers frequently lack reliable internet access.

The first travel idea is a **Flight Seat Comfort Comparison** that shows specific seat comfort information for exact flights including legroom, recline, power outlets, and window views based on crowdsourced data. Not all economy seats are equal and savvy travelers know this. An app that surfaces this information helps people choose better seats. Your prompt should be:

"Build a flight seat information app. Users search by airline and aircraft type to see seat maps with comfort ratings. Include data on legroom measurements, recline restrictions, power outlet availability, and proximity to lavatories and galleys. Allow users to contribute reviews of specific seats they've experienced. Show which seats are recommended and which to avoid for each aircraft. Design with a clean aviation inspired aesthetic using sky blue and white with clear aircraft diagrams."

Seat configuration data comes from various sources like SeatGuru, so respect their terms of service or build your database entirely from user contributions.

Second is a **Currency Converter with Offline Support** designed specifically for travelers who need reliable conversion without internet access. Basic currency apps exist but most require connectivity that international travelers often lack. This solves a real pain point. Prompt with:

"Create a currency converter app optimized for offline travel use. Users select home and destination currencies from a comprehensive list with flag icons. Enter amounts and see conversions instantly. Download exchange rates before traveling so conversions work offline. Include quick reference cards with common amounts pre-converted for easy market shopping. Support multiple currencies for complex trips. Design with a compact efficient interface using dark backgrounds with high contrast text for outdoor readability."

Exchange rates must be clearly timestamped so users understand that offline rates may be slightly outdated, and include prominent refresh functionality when online.

Third is a **Packing List Generator** that creates customized packing lists based on destination weather, trip duration, planned activities, and traveler preferences. Everyone forgets something when packing, and generic lists don't account for trip specifics. Smart generation solves this elegantly. Your prompt could be:

"Build a travel packing list app that generates customized lists. Users input trip details including destination, dates, and planned activities like hiking, business meetings, or beach time. The app generates a tailored packing list accounting for weather conditions during the travel dates. Allow editing the list, marking items as packed, and saving lists for future similar trips. Include common forgotten items with prominent placement. Design with an organized travel aesthetic using suitcase brown and white with satisfying checkmark animations."

Weather integration requires API access, so either integrate with a weather service or prompt users to input expected conditions manually.

Fourth is a **Jet Lag Recovery Planner** that provides a personalized schedule for adjusting to new time zones based on flight details and sleep science. Jet lag is physiologically complex but predictable, and research-backed adjustment strategies exist. This app makes them accessible. Your prompt should be:

"Create a jet lag management app based on sleep science. Users input their normal sleep schedule and flight details including departure and arrival times and time zones. The app generates a personalized adjustment schedule covering when to seek light, when to avoid light, optimal nap times, and recommended sleep times in the days before and after travel. Send timed notifications guiding users through the adjustment process. Design with a calm sleep-focused aesthetic using deep navy and soft white with celestial and circadian imagery."

The underlying science must be accurate, so source recommendations from peer-reviewed chronobiology research and include appropriate disclaimers about consulting doctors for medical advice.

Fifth in travel is a **Hidden Gems Local Guide** for specific cities featuring lesser-known restaurants, bars, and attractions recommended by actual locals rather than tourists. Guidebooks and major review sites steer everyone to the same overcrowded spots. Local knowledge is different and valuable. Prompt with:

"Create a local discovery app for finding hidden gems in Austin, Texas. Curate a collection of under-the-radar restaurants, bars, coffee shops, and attractions that locals love but tourists don't

know about. Each listing includes why it's special, best time to visit, what to order or experience, and practical details. Allow users to favorite spots and check-in when they visit. Include a map view showing all hidden gems. Design with a local zine aesthetic using hand-drawn typography and bold colors that feel authentically Austin."

Content creation is the main challenge since genuine local recommendations require actual local knowledge. Consider partnering with local content creators or building community contribution features.

Business & Professional Tools

Business and Professional Tools are where efficiency translates directly to money. The vibe is professional and all-in-one because business users want to solve complete problems rather than juggle multiple tools. These users have budgets and will pay real money for apps that save them time and increase their revenue.

The first professional tool idea is an **Appointment Booking System** for service professionals like barbers, stylists, massage therapists, and consultants who need clients to self-schedule. Phone tag between service providers and clients wastes everyone's time. Self-service booking is now an expectation. Your prompt should be:

"Build an appointment booking app for service professionals. Providers set up their services with duration and price, define their availability schedule, and share a booking link with clients. Clients browse available times and book appointments without needing an account. Send automated confirmation and reminder notifications to both parties. Include a calendar view for providers showing all upcoming appointments. Design with a professional but warm aesthetic using slate gray and soft gold that feels upscale and trustworthy."

Time zone handling is tricky since providers and clients may be in different zones, so ensure appointments are always displayed in the correct local time for each viewer.

Second is a **Simple Inventory Tracker** for small retail businesses or crafters who need to know what they have in stock, what's running low, and what to reorder. Full inventory management systems are overkill and overpriced for tiny operations. This fills the gap. Prompt with:

"Create a simple inventory management app for small businesses. Users add products with names, photos, current quantity, and minimum stock threshold. Track inventory changes through sales and restocking. Show alerts for items below minimum quantities. Include barcode scanning for quick lookup if possible. Generate simple reports on inventory value and movement. Design with a clean efficient interface using forest green and white that feels organized and businesslike."

Barcode scanning is a nice-to-have feature that adds significant complexity, so consider launching without it initially and adding based on user demand.

Third is an **Invoice Payment Tracker** that helps freelancers and small businesses track which invoices have been sent, which are overdue, and follow up on unpaid work. Getting paid is the hardest part of freelancing and organization helps significantly. Your prompt could be:

"Build an invoice tracking app for freelancers. Users add clients and create invoices with amounts, due dates, and status. Display a dashboard showing total outstanding, overdue amounts, and recently paid. Include status updates as invoices move from sent to paid. Generate follow-up reminder emails with one tap for overdue invoices. Show simple cash flow reports and payment history. Design with a professional financial aesthetic using navy blue and white with clear status indicators using green, yellow, and red."

Consider integration with invoicing apps to reduce double data entry, or include basic invoice generation capabilities to provide an all-in-one solution.

Fourth is a **Client Meeting Notes Organizer** that keeps all notes from client meetings organized by client and easily searchable for reference before future meetings. Professionals take meeting notes constantly but rarely have systems to find them later. This fixes that frustrating reality. Your prompt should be:

"Create a meeting notes app organized by client relationship. Users add clients and then create dated meeting notes under each client.

Include tagging for topics, action items, and decisions made. Before meetings, show recent notes and outstanding action items for that client. Make everything searchable across all clients and meetings. Include the ability to share specific notes via email. Design with a professional minimal aesthetic using charcoal and white with clear information hierarchy."

Note security matters since these notes may contain sensitive client information. Include passcode or biometric lock options and ensure notes are stored securely.

Fifth in professional tools is a **Simple CRM for Solopreneurs** that tracks leads and customer relationships without the overwhelming complexity of enterprise CRM systems. Full CRMs have hundreds of features that solo operators never use. Simplicity focused on solo needs creates a better experience. Prompt with:

"Build a simple CRM app designed for solopreneurs. Users add contacts with name, company, contact information, and source. Track relationship status through stages like prospect, active conversation, proposal sent, and customer. Log touchpoints like calls, emails, and meetings with dates and notes. Set follow-up reminders that trigger notifications. Show a pipeline view of all contacts by stage.

Design with a confident professional aesthetic using deep purple and white that feels capable but not overwhelming."

The balance between simplicity and capability is delicate because too simple feels useless and too complex defeats the purpose. Start minimal and add features based on actual user feedback.

There you have it. Fifty concrete app ideas spanning ten categories, each with clear prompts you can use immediately and considerations that separate amateur efforts from professional products. Remember that these ideas are starting points for your creativity, not rigid specifications. The most successful vibe coders take concepts like these and add their own twist, their own experience, their own understanding of a specific user need.

Choose an idea that genuinely excites you because that excitement will sustain you through the inevitable challenges of building and launching. Consider starting with the categories where you have personal experience since building for yourself first often leads to the best products because you understand the user deeply. Look at the considerations for each idea seriously because they represent the difference between apps that ship successfully and apps that get abandoned halfway through development.

Your fifty ideas are waiting. Your vibe coding tools are ready. The only question remaining is which one you'll build first.

About The Author

Marc Morales

Marc Morales is a tech & cyber enthusiast. He enjoys teaching about everything cyber and tech while maintaining a plethora of cyber-security & programming credentials. When he's not writing STEM books for younger readers, he's studying the latest trends in technology or writing cyber manuals and guides for older readers who have ambitions and goals.

If you enjoyed this book and learned a lot about vibe coding please consider leaving a positive review on Amazon or whichever platform you purchased this book from. Thank you so much!